MOUNTAIN
BIKING

D1383280

Meredith® Press

Des Moines, Iowa

Contents

Written by: Dan Hope

Studio photography: Polly Wreford

Location photography: Steve Behr

Art director: Jill Plank

Design co-ordinator: Graham Webb

Illustrator: Roy Avis

Production manager: Kevin Perrett

Managing editor: Miranda Spicer

Project manager: Kevin Hudson

Dan Hope has asserted his right to be identified as the author of this work.

First published 1995. This edition 1997
© Haynes Publishing 1995

Published by: Meredith Corporation
1716 Locust Street
Des Moines, IA 50309-3023

ISBN 0-696-20689-7

Printed in Italy by
G. Canale & C. S.p.A.
Borgaro T.se (Turin)

What is mountain biking?

Mountain biking was started by a few people who were looking for an exciting alternative to cycling along the road. It is now an international sport which anyone can pursue on any level, from being a professional racer to just going on an occasional family outing. Today, millions of people of all ages have discovered that mountain biking is incredibly fun to do, and highly addictive.

As the words suggest, mountain biking involves riding a bicycle through mountains. But it is not just this. The bikes themselves are designed to be ridden off-road, which means along trails, through woods, over rocks, across rivers – in fact anywhere that you want to go.

Once you have ridden a mountain bike off-road, you will understand what seasoned mountain bikers are talking about when they tell you about the thrill that they get from the sport. It combines the fun of riding a bike

with the excitement of speeding downhill, the satisfaction of stretching yourself physically and mentally, and the exhilaration of exploring beautiful countryside.

Not only is mountain biking an exciting activity, it is also an excellent way to see the world. You can cover huge distances and do not have to depend on anything other than yourself and your bike to get to your destination. And you do not have to worry about the terrain – a mountain bike will go anywhere.

Chapter 1

The mountain bike

Mountain bikes were first seen in Northern California in the early 1970s. They are now sold in their millions worldwide for a huge variety of uses. Their versatility enables them to be ridden over most kinds of terrain so they are equally at home in a rock-strewn, near-vertical gully or a traffic-filled street. Their robust go-anywhere looks have encouraged many potential couch-potatoes to become keen cyclists; whatever your age, sex, fitness and cycling ambition, you can just get on and ride.

What makes a mountain bike?

One of the first things you will notice about a mountain bike is its wide knobby tires. Another thing you will notice is its wide range of gearing–the standard is normally 21-speed derailleur gearing. A mountain bike also has a robust, relatively low-slung frame, designed to make a stronger and safer bike for riding on rough terrain and up and down hills. Together with powerful brakes, which will stop you quickly when you have been speeding downhill, these components make up a bike that can climb or descend almost anything.

Cantilever brake: robust and highly effective.

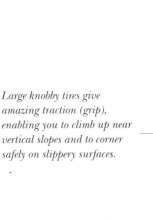

Large knobby tires give amazing traction (grip), enabling you to climb up near vertical slopes and to corner safely on slippery surfaces.

Drivetrain. Freewheel with seven sprockets combined with three chainrings provides 21 gears to cope with all manner of off-road terrain and gradient.

Flat handlebars for an upright riding position. Bar ends for an attacking position and generally going for it.

Gear shifters and brake levers mounted within easy reach. Enables vital split-second changes.

Low slung frame makes it easier to dismount from the bike in a hurry.

Suspension forks smooth out the bumps and provide relief to jarred elbows and arms.

Strong tubing and welding make a very robust frame. Tubing could be steel, aluminum or even titanium or carbon fiber.

Rugged, yet lightweight, wheels to withstand the pounding off-road.

Frames

The key element of a mountain bike is its frame. A good frame in the correct size will feel lively and will inspire confidence. A bad frame will feel sluggish and ungainly, and will not inspire you to ride to your limits. A mountain bike frame is more compact than that of a conventional bike, to increase rider stand-over height and safety, and to make it stronger.

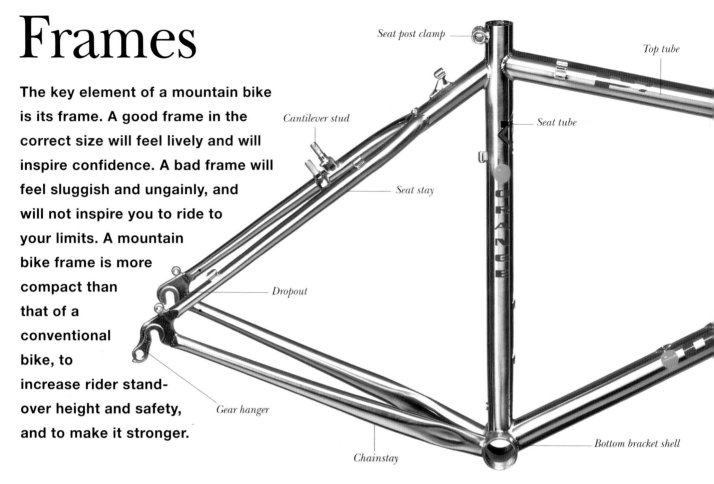

Seat post clamp
Top tube
Cantilever stud
Seat tube
Seat stay
Dropout
Gear hanger
Chainstay
Bottom bracket shell

Joining methods

TIG WELDING

The most widely used method of joining parts of the frame together is TIG (tungsten inert gas) welding. The parts are heated so that they fuse together with a filler metal (tungsten). The welding is carried out in an inert gas atmosphere to prevent impurities from affecting the weld. TIG welding does not use lugs which makes the bikes cheaper to produce.

BRAZING

Brazing is used for custom bikes, and only with steel. It is labor-intensive, which makes it expensive, but the end result is a smooth junction of tubes with no distinguishable joint. It forms a strong joint because it uses a filler material that has a low melting point, such as silver solder, and the tubing retains a high proportion of its original strength.

BONDING

Tubes made from materials that cannot be welded, such as carbon, are joined by bonding. Aluminum alloys, which cannot be welded without affecting their strength, are also bonded. The tubes are glued into lugs and the frame is put in an oven to set at a low temperature for several hours. The tubing retains a lot of its original strength and resilience.

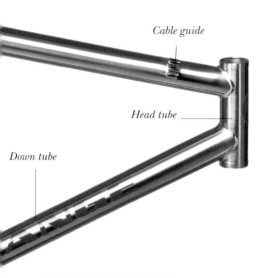

Cable guide

Head tube

Down tube

ORANGE P7 FRAME

This frame is made from lightweight Prestige tubing. It has a butted bottom bracket shell and head tube as well as main triangle. It has a nickel-plated finish.

FRAME SHAPE

Mountain bikes have to be very strong to cope with the rigors of off-road riding. Most mountain bike frames are diamond-shaped as bikes have been for 100 years. This gives strength to the frame because it is made up of triangles. The triangle is the strongest shape with which to build because it does not twist or break under pressure. It can be seen in many buildings and structures, for example in an iron railway bridge.

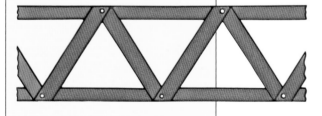

BUTTING

Tubes that are butted have a thicker wall at the ends than the rest of their length. The thickness reinforces the joints where strength may have been lost during brazing or welding, and keeps the rest of the tubes as light as possible where they do not require such strength. Steel is nearly always butted, and the process is also beginning to be used for more high-tech materials such as aluminum and titanium, but it makes these parts expensive.

WEIGHT AND STIFFNESS

Two important features that manufacturers have to consider when designing a frame are weight and stiffness. A stiff frame will allow the maximum amount of the rider's energy

to be converted into forward motion and the minimum amount will be wasted by the frame flexing. It is difficult to produce a lightweight frame that is also stiff, because to make a frame stiffer, the wall thickness of the tubes is increased. With the introduction of high-tech materials, the relationship between stiffness and weight is being improved all the time, but with higher costs.

Materials

Mountain biking is a very new sport and there is still scope for developing bike designs and materials. This has led to new designers, engineers and material specialists becoming interested in working with mountain bikes, and a huge range of materials normally used in other industries is being tried out.

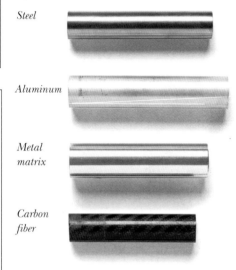

Steel

Aluminum

Metal matrix

Carbon fiber

STEEL

The material most widely used for mountain bike frames is steel. It is relatively cheap, very strong, and can be made quite light. It is usually TIG welded or brazed.

ALUMINUM

As technology increases, and alloys improve, aluminum is becoming more popular. It can be used to make a frame that gives a stiff ride or a compliant one.

METAL MATRIX

Most of these metals are alloys of aluminum with ceramic particles. They have an incredibly high strength-to-weight ratio, but their use in bikes has not yet been fully developed.

CARBON FIBER

This is a relatively new frame material, but potentially one of the best. It can be incredibly light but at the same time stiff and strong, and it has good shock-absorbing properties.

TITANIUM

A titanium frame is extremely light, incredibly strong and very expensive, due to the special welding required. Most titanium frames are said to have an almost infinite life span.

Drivetrain

The drivetrain transmits the power from your legs, when you pedal, to the back wheel, to propel the bike forwards. It comprises the crank arms, the chainrings, the chain, the freewheel and sprockets (cogs) and the gearing system. Mountain bikes have two shifters: one to move the chain on the chainrings and one to move it on the sprockets. Most mountain bikes have index gearing which means that the gear positions are synchronized, allowing you to shift, or change gear, in steps rather than by fine-tuning the position of the levers.

Freewheel with seven sprockets

Cable housing

Rear derailleur

Front derailleur

Three chainrings

Crank bolt

Chain

Shifters

STI SHIFTER
Shimano Total Integration (STI) shifters are mounted under the handlebars. They have two levers: one for shifting down with your thumb, and one for shifting up with your finger.

GRIP SHIFT
These shifters are mounted around the handlebars and are operated by rotation. You rotate towards you to shift into a lower gear, and away from you into a higher gear.

THUMB SHIFTER
The simple push-pull action and neat looks of thumb shifters make them popular with many riders. Sadly, no manufacturer produces high-quality ones any more.

CHAINS

The component of a mountain bike that probably takes more strain than any other is the chain. It has to stand up to a wide range of gearing and extreme gear changes, and is expected to work covered in mud, grit, water or sand. Manufacturers have responded to this by making chains far more flexible and by incorporating special plates that can stand up to these conditions.

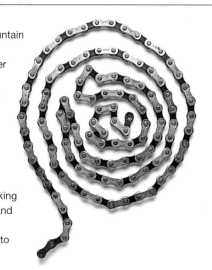

21-SPEED

This bike has a potential 21 gears obtained by using a combination of the chainrings and the rear sprockets. You would probably use all of these at some stage if you were riding off-road.

Chain cage

Crank arm

HYPERGLIDE CASSETTES AND CHAINS

When used together, these provide the smoothest gear changes on the market. The rear sprockets have 'ramps' and slanted teeth, which help guide the chain from one gear to another. A disadvantage is that the chain can only be joined with a special replacement pin. If incorrectly joined, it can break and can be difficult to rejoin. Shimano has also introduced Interactive Glide chains. These are a further improvement on Hyperglide chains.

DRIVETRAIN QUALITY

There is a huge choice when it comes to buying drivetrain components. Generally, an expensive setup will work better and last longer than a cheap one, but many affordable setups will shift perfectly well if they are assembled and maintained carefully. If you want to improve the shift quality of your drivetrain, consider changing the cables and chain first. Don't just put on more expensive derailleurs.

GEARING JARGON

• Gear ratio
The relationship between pedalling speed and wheel rotation speed, which depends on the gear selected by a chainring and rear sprocket combination. If the chain is on the largest chainring and smallest rear sprocket,

you are in the highest gear. If the chain is on the smallest chainring and largest rear sprocket, you are in the lowest gear.

• Cadence
The rate of pedalling, usually measured in revolutions per minute (rpm) of one foot. A high cadence is 120 rpm and a low

cadence is 60 rpm. You should aim to maintain a steady cadence. As a guide, the most efficient cadence is 80 rpm.

• Gear capacity
The maximum sprocket size that a front or rear derailleur can cope with. If a sprocket is too large, you can damage the derailleur.

Brakes

Mountain bikes can be ridden extremely fast – the world downhill speed record is more than 111 mph. It is therefore vital that these bikes are fitted with powerful and reliable brakes. The brakes need to work properly on rutted, loose and dusty trails in a multitude of different conditions, and must also offer good feel for better control. There are many different types of brakes, levers and brake pads available, but, if you are upgrading your system, remember that the effectiveness of your brakes also depends on the condition and material of your wheel rim, and the quality of your tires.

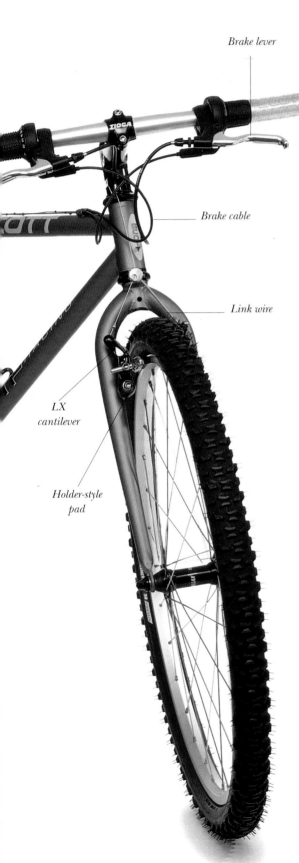

Brake lever

Brake cable

Link wire

LX cantilever

Holder-style pad

BRAKE BLOCKS
There is a wide variety of brake blocks, including holder-style blocks, which have removable pads. The current trend is to have pads with as large a surface area as possible to increase their grip. The pads can be made from plain rubber or a synthetic compound. Harder compounds do not wear as quickly as soft ones but they do not grip as well.

Aztec pads   *M-system pads*

BRAKE POWER
This Scott Comp Racing bike uses Shimano LX cantilevers to bring it quickly to a halt. These use holder-style brake pads, which are easily replaceable. They are operated by compact two-finger brake levers which need only a light action to provide serious stopping power.

Brake types

DISC

In specialist areas of mountain biking, such as downhill racing and speed-record attempts, disc brakes are becoming increasingly popular. Instead of using the rim as a braking surface, pads grip both sides of a large alloy disc attached to the hub. The main advantages of disc brakes are that they are far more powerful than anything else available and their effectiveness is not reduced by adverse conditions such as mud, snow and rain. They are more expensive than other types and require special attachments for the frame and forks. Alternatively, many top cross-country racers now use hydraulic brake systems, which use fluid instead of cables. The main reason for this is that they do not require any special attachments or hubs. They are significantly lighter than they used to be, and their feel and set up are improving all the time.

CANTILEVER

Most mountain bikes use cantilever brakes. These have good feel and power, and are mechanically simple. The pads are pushed on to the rim of the wheel by a system of pivots and springs when a connecting cable is pulled by the brake lever. They allow for a large amount of adjustment and can be set up in a variety of ways to get a different feel.

Brake levers

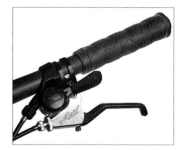

DIA-COMPE PC 7

This Dia-Compe brake lever is mounted separately from the shifter. You can therefore change the brake lever and shifter individually. It offers good feel and gives you extra braking power. This is because the cable goes through cams within the lever mechanism. When you have pulled the lever in to its full extent, the cable anchor point moves, pulling the cable farther.

SHIMANO ALIVIO

Most mountain bikes come fitted with Shimano brake levers and most of these use a system called Servo Wave. This is similar to the Dia-Compe system, providing extra braking power. Unlike the Dia-Compe lever, the Shimano brake lever is mounted on the same bracket on the handlebar as the gear lever. This means you cannot adjust their position independently from each other.

AVID

Avid was one of the first non-Japanese manufacturers to make a brake lever that offers more features and improved performance compared to the Japanese models. The Avid's features include adjustable barrel end placement, very lightweight construction, and excellent feel. They are very expensive due to the high number of special parts that they need.

TOE-IN

Brake blocks should be fitted at an angle so that the front of the blocks hit the rim of the wheel before the back. This angle is called the toe-in. It gives you a high degree of precision when varying your braking force, and helps to stop the brakes from squeaking badly.

Wheels

Mountain bike wheels are smaller than standard bike wheels, the diameter of the rim measuring 26 inches instead of 27. The smaller size gives them the necessary extra strength. At the center of the wheel is the hub, which contains the bearings on which the axle turns, and this is linked to the rim by spokes. All these components come in a range of quality and can be upgraded individually to provide improved performance, strength, resilience, aerodynamics and weight reduction.

Spoke

Hub

Axle

Rim

Spokes

The shape and strength of a wheel are dependent upon the spokes. There are usually 36 spokes in a wheel. It is a common misconception that spokes support the wheel in compression. They do in fact hold it in suspension. As the wheel turns, the hub hangs from the spokes that are attached to the rim at the top of the wheel.

nipple   *butting*   *spoke end*

SPOKE TYPES

The type of spokes can determine how the wheel responds to acceleration and downward force, which translates into feel to the rider. Spokes come in different lengths, gauges (thickness) and quality, but most are made from steel because this gives the best combination of strength and elasticity.

Three-cross pattern

SPOKE PATTERNS

These are arranged in a distinct cross pattern, usually between two- and four-cross. This refers to the number of times that one spoke is crossed by other spokes between the rim and the hub. Different riding characteristics can be obtained from the layout and type of spoke used in a wheel. Long heavy-duty spokes arranged in a four-cross pattern make a very strong wheel suitable for a heavy rider doing downhill racing. Lighter spokes with alloy nipples, arranged in a two-cross pattern would be suitable for a light person with more finesse.

Hubs

Mountain bike hubs need to be well sealed. Many have cartridge bearings or triple seals to prevent foreign objects from getting inside and creating havoc with the bearings. The hubs also need to be stiff and strong to reduce flex in suspension components and the frame. The use of oversized axles, with a greater contact area on the clamping surface of the hubs, is a common method of reducing flex. All bikes have a freewheel mechanism under the sprockets on the rear wheel, which allows the hub to turn freely in one direction. On mountain bikes this freewheel mechanism is usually built into the hub, rather than threaded on to the hub shell, and is called a cassette freewheel, or freehub.

Front hub – extra thick axle for use with suspension

Standard rear hub

Freehub body

Quick release skewer

Rims

It is important that mountain bike wheel rims have a good braking surface, are corrosion resistant and have a degree of resilience to stand up to the rocks, water and grit with which they will frequently come into contact. Aluminum wheel rims are best because they are lighter and more flexible than steel, and aluminum provides a better braking surface in the wet. The rims are normally made by extruding a large roll which is then cut down to size and joined by welding, pinning, or pinning and bonding. Wheel rims come in many different cross sections and finishes which can have specific uses.

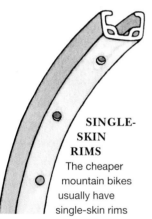

SINGLE-SKIN RIMS

The cheaper mountain bikes usually have single-skin rims because they are easier to make. The single layer of metal has to be fairly thick to make it strong enough, and the rims are therefore heavier than more expensive ones.

BOX-SECTION RIMS

The wheels of most mountain bikes have box-section rims, which have two layers of metal with a hollow area in between. This type of cross section increases the rims' stiffness, and also reduces their weight.

BOX-SECTION RIMS WITH MACHINED BRAKING SURFACE

Up until recently, wheel rims have not always had a consistent surface, which affected how the brakes performed. Now rims with a machined braking surface are available. This surface is hard and consistent and improves braking performance enormously.

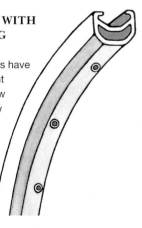

CERAMIC-COATED RIMS

Mountain bike wheel rims have a high wear rate caused by grit on the brake pads rubbing against them. Manufacturers have started to make some rims with a hard ceramic coating which lasts longer and also provides better friction. They are very expensive.

Tires

One of the main features of a mountain bike, which distinguishes it from a conventional bike, is its tires. These are generally much wider to increase traction and rider comfort, and have a large open-tread pattern for off-road riding. There is a large variety of tires available, and the type of tire you use is one of the most important factors that will determine how your bike performs.

INNER TUBES

Tire pressure is determined by the inner tube. Most mountain bike inner tubes are made from butyl. This is a combination of rubber and latex. Lighter inner tubes are made from latex. These are more puncture-resistant to certain types of puncture but they seep more than butyl and have to be pumped up more often. There are two main types of valve used on inner tubes. Schrader valves are the same sort of valves as used on car tires. Presta valves are specific bicycle tube valves. They allow more precise control over tire pressure but cannot be used with car air lines.

Butyl tube with Presta valve

Butyl tube with Schrader valve

TIRE CASING

There are two main types of tire casing. Cheaper mountain bike tires generally use what is called gumwall construction, which is heavy, but durable. The other, more popular, type is nylon casing, which is much lighter and more flexible, offering better cornering and traction. A nylon tire's casing quality is determined by the amount of TPI (threads per inch). The greater the TPI, the better the quality of tire.

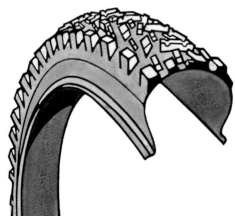

TIRE SIZE

Mountain bike tires come in different widths. A wide tire will give a more comfortable ride and increased traction in dry conditions. It will however be heavier and have increased rolling resistance, making the bike feel sluggish when accelerating. A narrow tire will be better at shedding mud and will have a lower rolling resistance, thus making it accelerate more quickly, but it will have less traction and give a less comfortable ride. When you buy tires, take into consideration your weight and riding style. If you are a light rider with a careful style, you can get away with narrower tires, but if you are a big, aggressive rider you will probably require wider tires, which will not puncture so easily.

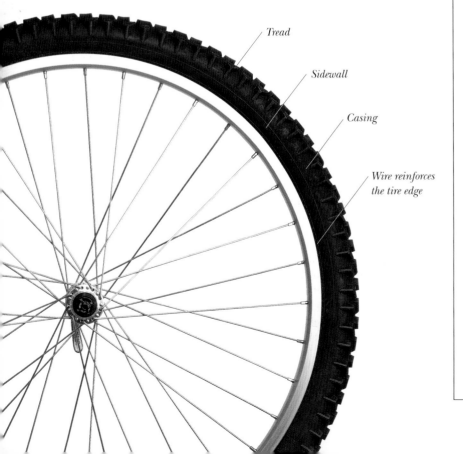

Tread

Sidewall

Casing

Wire reinforces the tire edge

Ritchey Cross Bite
Low rolling resistance and
inverted tread for good road use.

Ritchey Z Max
Excellent traction in soft conditions.
Not a general purpose tire.

Onza Rip/Rail
Specific tires for back and front
wheels. Front designed for
cornering, rear for traction.

Ritchey Red Z Max
Excellent lightweight cross-country
tire.

TIRE TREAD

Different tire treads are needed for different jobs. Completely smooth, or slick, tires are for road work, knobbies are for off-road riding, and multi-purpose are, as the name implies, for both road and off-road riding. Tread patterns vary to suit different conditions. For example, some are better in mud, some are more suitable for rock, and some provide better traction.

COMPOUND TIRES

There is a constant demand for improving tire performance, and tire manufacturers have responded by making tires with dual compounds. In these tires, the tread in the center is made from softer rubber than the side knobs, which need to be stiffer to increase stability. Many compounds are now sold specifically for use in mountain bike tires, especially downhill racing tires, which need to have excellent traction, stability and puncture resistance.

Ritchey Red Z Max/
soft compound tire

TREAD FOR FRONT AND REAR

Front and rear wheels do very different jobs, the back wheel needs traction and the front needs cornering control, so it is a good idea to have tires with different tread. Many mountain bike tires have directional tread. This gives you a choice of which way to orient a tire depending on the type of performance you want to get from it. Typically, a rear tire should face so the tread bites into the ground, and the front tire should be the other way around. Specific front and rear tires go a step farther. They have different tread patterns for their particular jobs.

Pedals

It is through the pedals that you power your bike forwards. Mountain bike pedals are generally wider than ordinary bicycle pedals and their surface ensures that your feet have a firm grip. Mountain bikes are sometimes fitted with toe clips and straps or clipless pedals, and these will improve your skill and boost your confidence in all off-road conditions.

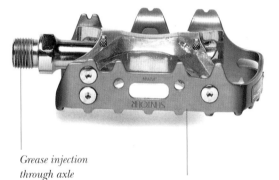

Grease injection through axle

Lightweight alloy construction

Toe clips and straps

Toe clips and straps are a very useful addition to a mountain bike pedal. They have several functions which greatly enhance performance and safety. Uphill and on the flat they increase your efficiency as you pull and push. Downhill they prevent your feet from sliding off the pedals in wet treacherous conditions and greatly enhance your bike control.

ADJUSTING A TOE STRAP

1 To tighten a toe strap, simply insert your foot and pull the strap upwards and towards you.

2 Once adjusted to the correct tension, the toe strap will remain in this positon.

3 Loosen the strap to dismount and before going downhill. Simply press outwards on the inner edge of the buckle.

BMX PEDALS

BMX pedals are increasingly popular for downhill, dual slalom and trials riding. Their broad platform and agressive tooth profile make them ideal for situations where grip is essential but where toe clips and clipless systems are not practical. You must protect your legs with shinpads if you use BMX pedals.

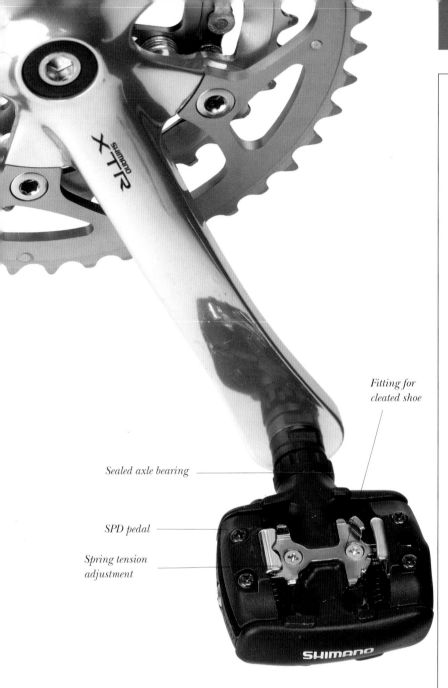

Fitting for cleated shoe

Sealed axle bearing

SPD pedal

Spring tension adjustment

Clipless systems

Clipless pedal systems such as Shimano's SPDs (Shimano Pedalling Dynamics) are the next step up from toe clips and straps. In any clipless system you have a shoe with a special attachment on the sole called a cleat. The cleat attaches to the pedal which means that you have no loss in efficiency through the pedal stroke, and you are totally at one with your bike in terms of control.

ADJUSTMENT

It is essential with any clipless pedal system that the cleat is set up in the right position in relation to your natural riding position. Incorrectly set-up cleats can cause knee problems. It is also important that you use your system's free float. When you are riding your foot will change position with the rotation of the pedal. Free float is designed to allow you that movement. Do not use up the free float in finding the natural position of your foot. It takes a fair amount of adjustment to find your ideal position.

GETTING ON AND OFF

To fix your shoe on the pedal, press down with the center of your foot, engaging the front part of the cleat, then press down hard with your heel, to click in. To remove your foot from clipless pedals, kick your ankle outwards, rotating your foot slightly. This method of removing your foot makes clipless pedals safer in a crash than toe clips and straps. When you crash your feet will probably rotate and will immediately come off the pedal.

CLIPLESS ADVANTAGE

Clipless pedals are increasingly popular. They can be used in mud, water and anything else you can throw at them, and once you are used to them they will give you the ability to lift the bike over obstacles on the trail and will help you get up hills more quickly.

PEDAL AND CLEAT

Most cycling shoes have holes drilled for cleats used in clipless pedal systems. When buying shoes, always check that they are compatible with the current clipless systems on the market. If you find it difficult positioning the cleats properly, get advice from the shop where you purchased them.

Suspension

The advantage you gain from having suspension on a mountain bike is that you can ride faster, farther and more comfortably with greater safety. There is a variety of systems on the market and most mountain bike ranges now include models with suspension of some sort. The technology is relatively new to mountain bikes, so manufacturers are still vying with each other to have their system recognized as the best.

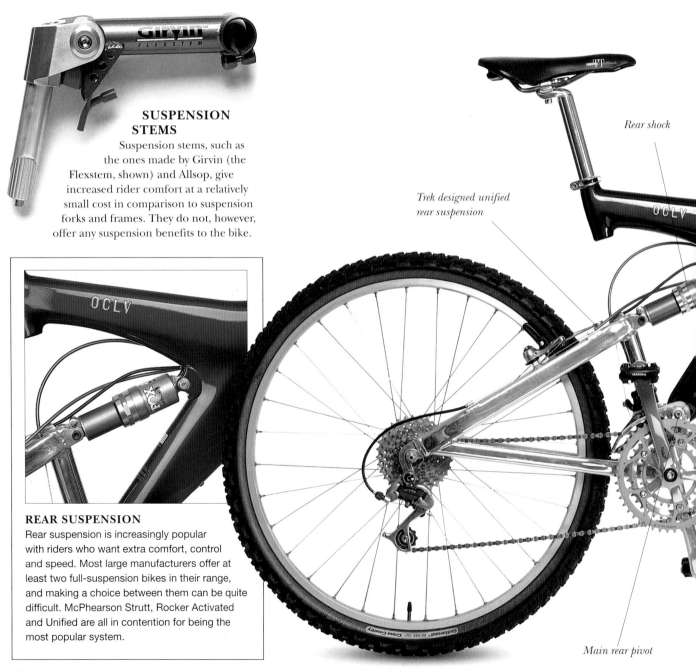

SUSPENSION STEMS
Suspension stems, such as the ones made by Girvin (the Flexstem, shown) and Allsop, give increased rider comfort at a relatively small cost in comparison to suspension forks and frames. They do not, however, offer any suspension benefits to the bike.

Rear shock

Trek designed unified rear suspension

REAR SUSPENSION
Rear suspension is increasingly popular with riders who want extra comfort, control and speed. Most large manufacturers offer at least two full-suspension bikes in their range, and making a choice between them can be quite difficult. McPhearson Strutt, Rocker Activated and Unified are all in contention for being the most popular system.

Main rear pivot

How suspension works

1 A suspension system comprises a spring and a damper. Suspension would be impossible without both. In principle, the spring supports the weight of the rider and the bike. When the bike hits a bump, the spring is compressed taking up the shock of the bump.

2 Once the bump has been absorbed, the compressed spring begins to stretch out again. The damper controls the rate at which this happens. Without damping, the spring would simply extend back at the same rate as that at which it was compressed.

3 The spring stretches back to its original length and the system is ready to absorb the shock from the next bump. The speed with which this happens dictates the feel of the ride and the damping characteristics can be altered depending on the type of suspension system.

Carbon fiber monocoque frame

Rock Shox Judy fork

Suspension forks

Mountain bike suspension forks are now highly developed and there are a lot of different makes and systems available. Telescopic forks are currently the most popular type for mountain bikes and the main choice lies in the type of spring damping unit used. The three main damping systems are oil/air, elastomer and elastomer/oil. Front suspension fork travel can be anything between 1 and 4 inches, depending on use.

Suspension front hub

The Trek Y33. Full active suspension and an OCLV carbon fiber monocoque frame. The ultimate ultra performance mountain bike.

Bars, stems and saddles

If you are to enjoy mountain biking to the fullest, it is important for you to have a suitable saddle and steering system. There is a huge variety of these components on the market and the ones you have on your bike can dramatically affect your comfort, control and safety. Most of them are fairly inexpensive and easy to change, and a few subtle adjustments to the way they are installed on to the bike can make all the difference.

Handlebars

Downhill upswept handlebar

Standard 3° handlebar

There are many different shapes and widths of handlebars available, and these will affect your riding position. Most mountain bikes have aluminum bars, which offer a fair degree of shock absorption, but steel, chromoly, carbon-fiber and titanium handlebars are also available. The more flexible the material of the handlebars, the more they will absorb vibrations when riding on bumpy trails. Bars are usually slightly bent on each side at an angle of between 3° and 5° so that they point inward towards the rider. Generally, women prefer slightly upswept handlebars with more inward sweep, whereas men prefer straighter handlebars which give a more aggressive riding position.

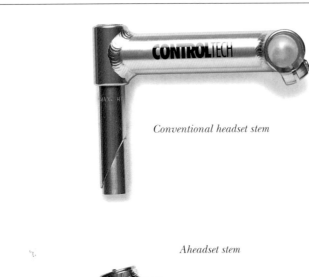

Conventional headset stem

Aheadset stem

Stems

The part that attaches the handlebars to the frame is called the stem. Like handlebars, mountain bike stems come in a variety of styles and materials. The length, height and angle will determine your riding position, and will affect how the bike feels and responds to your input. For example, if you put a short upright stem on your bike it will make the steering system much more precise at low speed, but more twitchy at high speed. A long flat stem will make the steering feel heavy at low speed, but will make it much more stable at high speed. Some stems have built-in shock absorbers, which make riding on rough trails easier on the hands and arms.

Headsets

The headset keeps the fork tube and stem inside the head tube of the bike frame. The upper and lower portions both contain ball bearings, allowing the steering system to move smoothly. There are three basic sizes: 2.5, 2.8 and 3 cm (1, 1 ⅛ and 1 ¼ inches). There are two different types – conventional headsets, which do up with a locknut, and a newer system called an Aheadset, which needs a special stem and fork, and is tightened using an Allen key. Aheadsets are lighter than conventional headsets, but provide far less scope for adjusting your riding position. They are generally used only on high-performance bikes.

Saddles

If you have had a bad experience with a saddle it can put you off cycling for life. There is now, however, a huge range of saddles available, varying in width, shape, material, weight and padding. When buying a saddle or bike, ask the shop if you can try the saddle for a few days and if you find it uncomfortable exchange it for another.

NARROW SADDLE

It is a common misconception that narrow saddles are uncomfortable, and many people prefer narrow saddles. They are good when riding off-road because they enable you to slide off the back of the saddle easily for descending.

WIDE SADDLE

If you do a lot of riding when you are constantly sitting on the saddle, you may want a slightly wider saddle and a greater depth of padding. Do not make the mistake of buying a saddle that is too wide, because it may rub the inside of your thighs.

Grips

Handlebar grips need to be able to absorb vibrations and give good grip in a variety of conditions. There are many different types of grip available: they can be made from types of foam, rubber or gel material, and most styles come in different diameters. You may have to try several types before you find one that you are comfortable with.

WOMEN'S SADDLE

Most women have a wider pelvis than men and so find saddles that are wider at the back more comfortable. Women's saddles, like men's, are available in different widths and designs for different uses.

Bar ends

A great addition to mountain bike handlebars are bar ends. These are handlebar extensions which bolt on to the end of the handlebars or are fitted inside the ends. They give you the benefit of being able to hold the handlebars in different places and so alter your riding position during long rides, and prevent your hands from going numb. They also make it easier to climb hills because your weight is distributed better over the front wheel when you hold them. Bar ends come in different designs and materials.

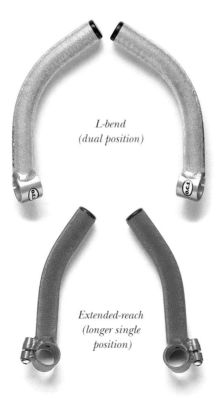

L-bend
(dual position)

Stubby
(single position)

Extended-reach
(longer single position)

CHAPTER 2

The right bike for you

With so many different mountain bikes – and components – to choose from, you can be excused for wondering how you will know which one to get. Buying one that is the right size is obviously a good idea, but it is also important that you get a bike that suits your riding style and ability. Once you have chosen the correct bike, you can then make several minor adjustments to perfect the bike for you. You will soon gain the confidence and inspiration to ride anywhere.

The basic essentials

When choosing a bike, the main thing is to look for one that is suitable for you and the type of riding you want to do. Manufacturers normally put their bikes into different categories: entry-level (bikes aimed at the first timer), mid-range (bikes aimed at semi-serious enthusiasts) and pro-racing (quality bikes aimed at people who want to compete). The bike shown here is fitted with the type of components you should expect to find on a mid-range bike from any manufacturer.

BEFORE YOU BUY A BIKE

• Set yourself a budget so that you look at bikes only within your range. Do not forget that there are some essentials that you will have to buy, such as a helmet, lock and lights.

• Consider how often you are going to ride the bike and what type of riding you intend to do.

• Collect sales literature on the current bikes to find out what models are on the market and what the differences are between similar models from different manufacturers.

• Arrange to have a test ride on the ones you like the look of.

• If you want a secondhand bike ask a knowledgeable person to check a bike's road-worthiness. Ask the seller for original purchase receipts, to make sure that the bike is not stolen. Try to establish what type of riding the bike has been used for, to make sure that it has not been thrashed.

DERAILLEURS
Shimano derailleurs currently offer the best-quality gear shifts on the market. The bike should have the best derailleurs available within its price bracket.

CONTACT POINTS

As the name suggests, these parts are the ones with which you will be in contact when riding your bike, ie the saddle, handlebars, grips and pedals. Make sure that these are all comfortable for you.

GEARS

Look for indexed gears. These make gear shifting easy, because all you have to do is click the lever into the next position.

BRAKES

A mid-range mountain bike should have cantilever brakes. They are far more powerful than conventional caliper brakes. If possible, get M-system pads because these are very good in the wet.

RIMS

It is very important that your bike has alloy wheel rims. These are much easier to restraighten than steel rims, are much lighter and perform better in the wet.

FRAME

The best mid-range mountain bike to get is one with chromoly tubing. Chromoly is very strong, quite light and relatively inexpensive. The two most common manufacturers of chromoly tubing are Tange and True temper.

CRANK-SET

In order for your mountain bike to climb hills, it requires a triple crank-set. This should give you enough gears to make it possible for you to climb up anything.

TIRES

Check that the tires are the right kind for the type of riding you will be doing. Road tires are not suitable for off-road and vice-versa.

Today's mountain bikes

Mountain bikes range from all-round off-road bikes through to top-of-the-range, custom-built racing bikes. Ask a shop to advise which is the best type for you. You probably don't need to get the latest, most expensive model on the market, especially if you are a beginner at the sport. If you want to, you will be able to adjust and upgrade most of the bike's components later, to suit your own particular needs and style of riding.

MID-RANGE BIKES

If you are intending to use your bike purely for off-road use, a mid-range bike would be the most appropriate for you. It is in the middle of their range that manufacturers make bikes aimed at off-road riders. The frames and components begin to be lighter and more durable. You will be able to get good value for money with a mid-range bike because this part of the range is the most competitive area for mountain bike manufacturers.

OFF-ROAD RACING BIKE

This Scott Comp Racing bike has a lightweight chromoly frame. It has a long top tube, a steeper angled seat tube than normal and a saddle higher than the handlebars. These things put the rider into an aggressive racing position.

ALL-ROUND BIKE

The Trek 930 will cope with a huge variety of off-road terrain. Its geometry is suited to recreational riding and touring because it offers a fairly upright riding position. A large amount of adjustment is possible in the stem and seat position.

Vetta saddle

21-speed gearing

21-speed Grip Shift

Sloping top tube

Hand-built TIG-welded frame

Vetta saddle

Rugged frame

Bar ends as standard

24-speed Grip Shift

Steep seat tube

Clipless pedals
as standard

Ritchey tires

Tioga Psycho tires

24-SPEED
The 24-speed drivetrain offers a very wide range of gears. This allows you to   keep up an even pedalling cadence through gear changes.

AHEADSET STEM
This system reduces the weight of the front end of the bike which is an advantage on a racing bike. You can flip the stem to offer another riding position.

Aheadstem

Hand-built wheels

Rock Shox fork

TREK 7000 SHX
This high-performance recreational bike is constructed from Easton aluminum 7000-series tubing, which gives it a stiff, light frame. The frame has been designed to accommodate a suspension fork.

Middle to top of the range

Bikes in the mid- to top-range can vary quite a lot depending on how the manufacturer has wanted to spec the bike and for what kind of use it has been designed. Some will come with a suspension fork or a lightweight alternative. The top bikes will be 24-speed and made of high-tech materials.

BONDED TUBING
The tubing of this 7000 SHX is bonded. The main benefits of this are that the bike has a very correct alignment and minimum heat distortion.

SUSPENSION FORK
This Trek bike has a Rock Shox suspension fork. This increases the height of the front end fractionally, and the bike has a low stem to allow for this.

CUSTOM TUBING
A feature of Pace frames is their custom extruded box-section aluminum tubing. This makes the frame extremely light and also very strong.

EXTERNAL BUTTING
The external butting process used on its tubing gives this frame added strength and reduces its weight and gives it its unique look.

SOPHISTICATED FORK
Pace manufactures its own suspension fork with a rear-mounted brake. It is a mixture of carbon fiber, aluminum and special chromoly, and is one of the most sophisticated suspension forks on the market. Its dual brace and box-section crown give it incredible stiffness.

PACE F4
Pace is a small, specialty frame manufacturer. It is the only company to manufacture its own tubing.

Sloping top tube

One-piece stem/steerer tube reduces overall weight

Mavic rims

Anti-chain-suck device prevents frame damage

Children's bikes

Mountain biking is one of the few sports in which the whole family can take part together. Children love riding bikes, and with a mountain bike they can get off the streets and away from traffic. There are many good children's mountain bikes now available, and they can be adjusted in the same way as adults' bikes. Some offer the same features as adult ones, which make them even more fun for children to ride.

CORRECT SIZE

A child should have 3 to 4 inches of clear space between her crotch and the top tube when she straddles the middle of the bike, with feet flat on the floor. Do not buy a bike that is too big just because it will last for several years. The bike should fit the child now.

The child must have the correct reach on the bike so as not to be too cramped or too stretched out.

SMALL ADULT'S BIKE

Most large mountain bike manufacturers make sizes as small as 35 cm (14 inches) in their adult bike range. This is a 41.25 cm (16½-inch) Trek 850 with full-size wheels. This is a good way to buy a bike for an older child who is confident at riding. It gives plenty of scope for seat post and stem adjustment as the child grows.

The correct-size frame should last for several years.

CHILD SEAT

You can carry a child of up to about five years old, depending on his or her weight, in a child seat. The best type to get is one that has a high head rest. It should also have a safety belt and adjustable foot buckets with straps to keep the child's feet in.

Make sure that your child always wears a helmet that complies with safety standards when riding a bike.

The child must have the correct reach on the bike so that he or she is not too cramped or too stretched out.

Use the adjustable-reach screw to position the brake levers closer to the handlebars.

Six-speed derailleur.

Reflectors should be mounted on the pedals, wheels and on the front and back of the bike.

CHILD'S BIKE

This is a child's bike made by Scott. It is an exact scaled-down version of one of their adult bikes. Its features include a six-speed Grip Shift, cantilever brakes and alloy rims with off-road tires.

Upgrading your bike

The majority of low- to mid-range bikes come with only basic parts such as all-round tires and wide saddles. Most manufacturers save their more sophisticated parts for their top bikes. You do not have to buy a top-of-the-line bike to get good performance, however. You can easily turn your basic mountain bike into a serious off-road machine, although this may be more expensive in the long run.

Narrower saddle makes it easier to shift your weight back for steep drop-offs.

Knobby tires improve climbing and braking ability.

AS YOU LIKE IT
One of the best things about upgrading is that you can personalize your bike. Shops are brimming over with the latest accessories, which are relatively easy to install.

CLIPLESS PEDALS
Putting on clipless pedals is a fairly expensive upgrade, because you will have to buy special shoes too, but the performance advantages that they will give you are huge. You will be able to get in and out of the pedals quickly, you will have 100 percent connection with the pedals to limit energy wastage, and your feet will be secure on the pedals in even the worst conditions. The pedals also give you plenty of clearance off the ground, which is essential for tight cornering. The best clipless pedals are made by Shimano, Ritchey, Tioga and Onza. Once you have tried some, it is unlikely that you will ever go back to using conventional pedals.

Bar ends help on long rides.

Lowered stem gives a more aggressive riding position, which will help to keep the front wheel on the ground when you push hard through a corner.

Two water bottles for strenuous off-road riding.

Heavy-duty, alloy water bottle cages keep bottles secure on bumpy trails.

Toe clip and strap.

BAR ENDS

Put bar ends on your bike to increase your ability to ride powerfully out of the saddle. If you hold the bar ends on a steep climb you will put more weight on the front wheel and stop it from lifting off the ground.

TOE CLIPS AND STRAPS

You will find that toe clips and straps will help you to climb uphill, and will prevent your feet from slipping off the pedals when you go downhill. They can also help you when bunny hopping the bike on a trail. Get used to them before taking on a serious off-road ride.

SADDLES

It can be a good idea to install a new saddle when you buy a bike, to tailor it to the type of riding you want to do. A narrow saddle such as this Vetta Tri Shock is comfortable and will allow you to slide off the back, when doing steep off-road descents.

TIRES

Most entry-level and mid-range mountain bikes come with tires that are designed for all-round off- and on-road riding. For serious off-road riding, install a more knobby tire. This Ritchey Z Max will give you the best in off-road traction you can get.

Super bikes

Most mountain bike manufacturers make enthusiast bikes aimed mainly at experienced racers. As with super cars, these super bikes involve a great deal of creative design input and generate a huge interest among mountain bike devotees. Only a small number of each model is made so they are more expensive than the top-of-the-line mass-produced bikes, but they are the best you can get.

6000 Series aluminum tubing

GT triple triangle frame design

Onza clipless pedals

Replaceable dropout

GT ZASKAR

The GT Zaskar is hand-built in the USA from 6000-series aluminum and is available in a variety of built-up and frame-only options. This one is built-up with a selection of top-line components parts from manufacturers such as Rock Shox, Onza and Mavic. It is virtually indestructible and therefore ideally suited to hard cross-country racing and general trail thrashing.

Odyssey lever

SCOTT PRO RACING

This bike is an exact replica of the one on which Gary Foord has won numerous Grundig World Cup races. The Scott Pro Racing is built from very lightweight chromoly steel tubing. Its overall built-up weight is about 22.5 pounds, making it one of the lightest bikes with a suspension fork.

Cook Bros. cranks

Lightweight chromoly steel tubing

Soft compound Ritchey tires

TREK OCLV PRO ISSUE

Trek has based the OCLV Pro Issue on the bikes ridden by their successful professional racers, such as former world champion Don Myrah. Its carbon fiber frame is currently the lightest production mountain bike frame on the market, weighing in at a mere 2.88 pounds.

Carbon fiber frame

Rock Shox SL forks

XTR group

Continental tires

GT LTS

It may look outlandish, but it works. The GT LTS is one of the best downhill racing bikes on the professional circuit, and those who ride it are difficult to beat. It is also one of the best suspension bikes currently available, with more than 3 inches of active travel.

Gusseted top tube

Fox rear shox

Downhill front suspension forks

Hand-built aluminum frame

Buying a bike

When you decide to buy a bike, check out as many shops as possible. Buy your bike from the shop that you find most helpful, that has a good selection to choose from, and that offers a good back-up service. When you have chosen a particular bike, check it all over to make sure that eveything is in good working order. This will avoid your having to bring the bike back and could prevent you from having a serious accident.

THE SHOP

Bike shops come in many different forms, from very high-end to very basic. Try to find one that will give you good post-sale service and will help you later with any problems that you may have. Bikes always require a certain amount of setup and adjustment after they have been bought.

Test riding

1 Check the frame size for the correct leg extension (see p. 42). You should not have the saddle above the maximum height mark on the seat post.

2 Check that you are not too stretched out or cramped up. Your arms should be relaxed but at the same time should feel poised for action.

3 Check how the bike responds under hard acceleration when you are riding out of the saddle. If the bike is not right, the steering will feel skittish and unstable.

Pre-purchase checks

1 Check that the front wheel is secure in the forks and that the quick-release lever is done up tightly.

2 Check that the headset feels tight. It can affect your warranty on the bike if you ride while the headset is loose.

3 Push hard down on the handlebars while riding the bike, to make sure everything feels tight and solid.

4 Check that the handlebar stem is correctly tightened in the frame. If it is not, it could result in a bad accident.

Helpful hints on buying

• Compare brands and models before you buy. Do not get pushed into a quick deal without knowing everything about a bike.
• Double-check that you are buying the right size.
• Check that you are not paying more than the current retail price for the model.

• Ask the retailer why they are selling at such a low price if something seems a particularly good deal. The bike may have a defect, and have lost its warranty.
• Take up any offer of a free 30-day tune-up with the bike, because this service is very important for the life of the parts.

• Take a knowledgeable friend with you to ask any useful questions that you may not have thought of and explain any jargon that you might not understand. Always make a point of asking as many questions as possible and if the salesperson is not helpful, go somewhere else.

Which size?

Finding the right type of mountain bike is quite easy, but getting the right size is not as simple. When you ride a bike that is the correct size, and properly set up, you will feel relaxed and comfortable, and you will be able to tackle rough trails and slopes with confidence. As you gain more experience of mountain biking you may find you want to make some adjustments to the bike, to give you a different riding position, and this is easily done.

ADJUSTING SADDLE HEIGHT

Mountain bikes generally have a higher bottom bracket than other bikes so you will be riding slightly higher on it. Start with the seat low, and raise it as you gain confidence. As a guide to the right height, you should be able to reach the pedal with your heel, with your knee straight, when the pedal is at its lowest point.

FINDING THE RIGHT SIZE BIKE

To find a bike that is the right size, first straddle the center of the top tube. You should have 3 to 4 inches between you and the top tube with your feet flat on the floor. Then try the length. With the saddle in the middle position on the seat post, and the handlebars at the same height, you should be able to sit on the bike comfortably without straining. If you are too stretched out when you are riding, you will be unbalanced and have less control. If you are too cramped up, you will feel as if your knees are going to hit your stomach. Another good indication that a bike is too small is if you have to push the seat post and stem above their maximum height markings to give you a comfortable riding position. If you ride a bike like this, the seat post and stem can come out and you could have a bad accident.

THE FRAME SIZE MESS

One of the most difficult things about buying a bike and getting the correct size, is that manufacturers use different criteria when stating bike sizes. Most manufacturers make their bikes with a fixed relationship between the seat-tube length and the top-tube length, so if you cannot find one make of bike that fits, try another. Do not expect one 19-inch bike to be the same as another.

TOO BIG
If your bike is too big, you will not be able to jump off easily in an emergency which can be dangerous.

TOO SMALL
If your bike is too small you will be cramped on it, and it will give you an uncomfortable ride.

ADJUSTING SADDLE POSITION

You will probably have approximately 2 inches of fore-and-aft adjustment on the rails of your saddle. Try the saddle in different positions until you find the most comfortable one. Again, as a guide, with your foot on the pedal, your knee joint should be above the pedal axle when the crank arm is pointing forwards horizontally.

ADJUSTING HANDLEBARS

The height of most stems can be adjusted by 1 to 2 inches. Try different positions until you find the one that gives you the ideal riding position – with your back at a 45° angle and your arms slightly bent. For most people, the handlebars are best 1 to 2 inches lower than the saddle.

A correctly sized bike – 3 to 4 inches clearance over top tube

Perfecting the fit

Once you have found the right bike in the right size, and made the necessary alterations to improve your comfort, you can make more minor adjustments to perfect the fit. These can make a big difference in how easy the bike is for you to ride. It is possible that you may not be able to position a component exactly as you want it. If so, try a different one. You are bound to find one that suits you.

CHANGING PARTS

If you have problems perfecting the fit, and have to change a component, try to do this when you buy the bike, because this normally works out cheaper.

Saddle

It can take a while to find the perfect saddle. As with shoes, you may find one brand that is more comfortable for you than others. It is important that you do not have too much padding in the saddle. Far from being more comfortable to sit on, it is actually less comfortable because it will rub your thighs more. Do not get one that is too wide either. This will make it difficult for you to slip off the back before descending a steep slope.

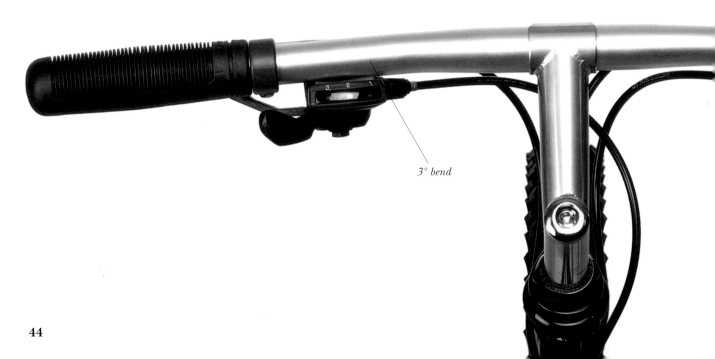

3° bend

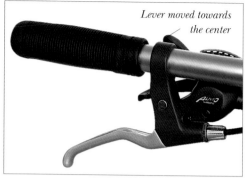

Brake levers

Most levers are attached to the handlebars with an Allen key clamp. By loosening this clamp, you can make several adjustments to the position of the brake lever to make it more comfortable to use.

Lever moved towards the center

IN AND OUT

You can move the levers farther towards the grips or towards the center of the bar. This position depends on your shoulder width.

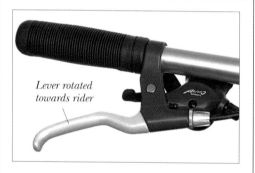

Lever rotated towards rider

UP OR DOWN

You can rotate the levers up or down, so that they suit how your wrists and hands sit on the handlebars.

Smaller reach between lever and handlebar

REACH ADJUSTMENT

You can move the static resting position of the brake levers, nearer or farther away from the handlebars according to whether you have small or large hands. The brakes may need additional setting up after this adjustment.

Stem

HANDLEBAR STEM

If you cannot put the handlebars currently on your bike into a position which is comfortable, change the stem. They are available in a variety of rise angles, lengths and quill lengths (the part of the stem that fits into the fork).

Handlebars

Most handlebars bend backwards at an angle of between 3° and 5°. You can rotate the bars a small amount in the stem clamp to move the position of the angled ends up or down. The best position is simply the one that feels most comfortable.

CHAPTER 3

Clothes and accessories

As with any sport, you will get the most out of mountain biking if you and your bike are suitably outfitted. Some accessories are essential, but many of the amazing selection of gadgets you see advertised are useful only in certain conditions. Get to know your bike and what you want to do with it, then you can enjoy gradually adding things to it that you really need. Similarly, you don't have to buy all the special clothing, but bear in mind that much of it is designed to make cycling safer, easier and more comfortable.

Helmets

Your head is the most vulnerable part of your body when cycling and should be protected. Always wear a helmet when you are cycling, both on- or off-road. In some states it is compulsory. A helmet is especially necessary when you are riding in rocky unknown terrain, because this is when you can easily have a crash. The main thing to check when buying a helmet is that it meets the safety standards set and tested by institutes such as Snell or ANSI (in the US), Eu (Europe), BSI (Britain) or AS (Australia). This will be marked inside the helmet.

CHILD'S HELMET
Many children's helmets have colorful designs on them to appeal specifically to children. These may encourage children to wear a helmet but, whatever the design, the helmet should meet one of the recognized safety standards. Brightly colored helmets show up more, and this may help other road users to see a child. Be careful with stickers. Only use ones that are approved for helmets.

CHILD'S HELMET FRONT VIEW
It is important that you buy a helmet that fits your child now. Do not buy one for the child to grow into, because a badly fitting helmet will give very little protection. The helmet should sit low on the head without obstructing vision, and should fit snugly so that you cannot move it from side-to-side.

HELMET LIFE
In the event of a crash, always have a helmet inspected by the shop that sold it to you. It may well have been rendered useless, even if you cannot see any damage. Bicycle helmets are designed to withstand one major impact only. Also do not leave your helmet in direct sunlight or near strong chemicals.

SIDE VIEW
The helmet should protect the back of the child's head as well as the forehead. Adjust the strap so that it fits snugly under the chin, preventing the helmet from moving out of position. The 'joint' should be just under the ears. Avoid pinching the child's skin in the snap-lock buckle if you do it up for her, because this is extremely painful. Always ask her to hold her chin up.

TOO BIG
If the helmet sits so low on your head that it obstructs your vision, it is too big. If you can move it backwards and forwards and from side-to-side, it is too big.

TOO SMALL
If a helmet looks perched on the top of your head, it is too small. If it pinches the sides of your head and feels uncomfortable, it is too small.

BACKWARDS
With so many new helmet designs on the market it is easy to wear one backwards, as shown here, and the helmet will then not protect your head properly.

OUTSIDE
Helmets can have a soft or hard outer shell, or a thin outer shell called a microshell.

ADULT'S HELMET FRONT VIEW
A helmet should fit your head like a glove. You should be able to feel the helmet on the top of your head and it should move with your scalp when you wiggle your eyebrows. It should fit low on your forehead without obstructing your vision to the front or to the side.

INSIDE
Most helmets come supplied with padding for the inside. This will enable you to adjust the helmet to suit your head shape. This padding is normally attached with Velcro for easy installation and removal.

HELMET TYPES
There is a huge range of styles, colors and fits of helmet available. Look for a lightweight helmet which has good ventilation, but choose a style that fits you well, and in which you feel most comfortable. Most helmet manufacturers offer between two and five different shell sizes.

SIDE VIEW
You should wear a helmet so that it is level, not too far forwards or backwards. The straps should be tight enough so that they fit snugly under your chin and will prevent the helmet from moving around on your head while you are cycling.

Dressing for comfort

It is a basic fact that if you are not comfortable you will not enjoy yourself, and if you wear unsuitable clothes or shoes, you can finish the day blistered and bruised. You don't have to wear 'spray-on-look' Lycra. There is a large range of functional loose-fitting clothes available if you prefer a more relaxed, non-racer look.

Practical clothes

Heavy-duty sweatshirt

Cotton racing jersey

Loose-fitting shorts with padded insert

Lycra shorts

SHIRTS
These are designed not to leave exposed areas of skin when you are stretched forward on your bike. They are longer in the arm than normal shirts, and are cut longer over the back. They are available mainly in cotton-blend fabrics, which have a nice feel.

SHORTS
You can buy loose-fitting shorts with a padded insert for comfort. They come in a variety of plain earth colors and are usually quite acceptable in shops and restaurants.

CYCLING SHORTS
If there is one piece of clothing that would really make an improvement to your enjoyment of cycling, it is a pair of cycling shorts. They are the most comfortable shorts in which to ride, and are available in different fabrics. They should fit snugly but not so tightly that they cut off your circulation.

Shoes

ALL-PURPOSE SHOE
This Nike Nguba shoe has a stiff sole that is SPD compatible, and it is not too stiff to walk in. It is a 'half boot' so it gives your ankle bone some protection.

SERIOUS SHOE
The Axo Pony is aimed at the serious mountain biker. It has a very stiff sole and a reinforced toe cap to prevent you from stubbing your toes.

RACING SHOE
The racing version of the Axo Pony, the Axo Mission has a lower cut and an extremely stiff sole. It has a reinforced toe and fastens with laces and Velcro for security.

Gloves

TRADITIONAL GLOVES
Short-fingered gloves are good for cycling because they allow you more control. These knitted gloves are popular because they have excellent ventilation.

TOP OF THE RANGE
These Trek Elite gloves are the best short-fingered gloves around. They are so comfortable you will hardly know you are wearing them.

RACING GLOVES
These gloves are made from Amara, which is an artificial leather, and Lycra. The advantage of Amara is that unlike leather it stays pliable after washing. Lycra improves the ventilation.

EYE PROTECTION
When riding a bike it is very important to protect your eyes from flies, mud, ultra-violet light and dust. Racers like to wear glasses because they hide their emotions and make them look mean. There are a number of different types of glasses available, with different types of lenses for different conditions. Yellow or orange lenses are good on gray days and at night. Iridium lenses are good for reducing glare on very bright days.

Sub Zeros with amber lenses for dull light

Dark lenses in M Frame for general bike use

M Frame with Iridium-coated lenses for bright sunlight

0.4 Sub Zeros, fashionable for use on and off the bike

Technical clothing

For serious excursions you will need clothing for a wide range of weather conditions. During one day's off-road riding, you may experience wind, rain, sun and extreme temperature changes as you change altitude and ride through sheltered then exposed areas. There are many fabrics and garments, commonly described as technical, that are designed specially for these conditions.

JACKET
Technical jackets are made from a fabric that is waterproof but can breathe. They fit the body closely to reduce wind resistance, have long arms and are long at the back. Some have zips under the arms for ventilation.

THERMAL SHIRT
In cold weather, wear a thermal shirt, which will keep your body heat in. Garments that go against your skin are known as base layer clothing. They should be made from fabric that breathes and wicks (absorbs sweat and lets it evaporate). It is essential that, for these special fabrics to work, every layer of clothing is made from them.

RACE JERSEY
Good race jerseys are made from fabrics such as Coolmax and Fieldsensor. Both these fabrics have excellent breathing abilities and keep the wind out. It is useful if they have rear pockets in which you can keep food and spare clothing.

SOCKS AND GLOVES
It is normally your hands and feet that suffer most in the cold and wet. Good socks and gloves are therefore important things to have, and both are now available in technical fabrics.

BALACLAVA

Wear a balaclava in extreme winter conditions. It will reduce the heat loss through your head, which will be a big help in keeping you warm. If you get a thin one you will still be able to wear a helmet.

HELMET

The best helmets have features such as Coolmax foam padding to keep your head cool, and more air vents than cheaper models. Some will also have built-in Kevlar roll cages.

SHORTS

If you are doing a lot of riding, it is essential to wear a good pair of Lycra cycling shorts. The best ones are made from eight panels of fabric and are cut in such a way that they will still fit your leg when it is bent.
Lycra is an ideal fabric for shorts because it is both supportive and has the ability to wick and dry.

For your bike

There are many useful bike accessories on the market, which will make your trips even more enjoyable. Some of these are just fun to have, others are essential for certain types of ride, for example when you are cycling off-road at night, or going on a long day trip. Most good mountain bike shops will have these accessories in stock and will be able to advise you but, as you ride more, you will find out what you need.

10-watt halogen front light

BIKE BAGS

There are several types of bag in which you can carry essential items when riding. One of the neatest ways is in a seat pouch. These are available in a variety of sizes, and can take a surprising amount of tools, clothes and spare parts necessary for a day's outing. The best ones have a clip system with which to attach them to the base of the seat. They can be taken on or off quickly and easily.

Handlebar-mounted bags are also available. They hold more than a seat pouch and most allow you to carry a map on the top, underneath a see-through waterproof cover. This means you do not have to stop for too long to find out where you are going and can even map read while you are riding along.

LED rear light

LIGHTS

Riding off-road at night can be great fun if you have some powerful lights. There are now many systems on the market with 10-watt lamps, which give you great visibility. (Normal bike lights are usually only 2.5-watt.) They will last for two or three hours. LED lights are increasingly popular for road riding because they have a three-to-four-month battery life and most are light and compact to carry.

2.5-watt front light with adjustable focus

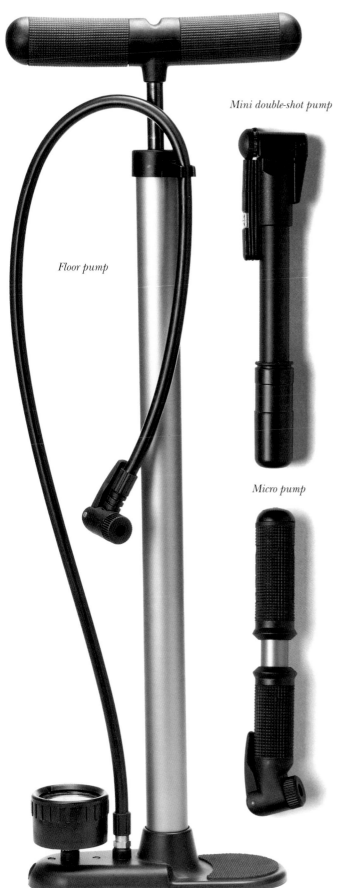

Mini double-shot pump

Floor pump

Micro pump

WATER BOTTLES

The capacity of water bottles varies from 0.75 liter (1.3 pint) to 1.5 l (2.6 pint). Most bottles are made of plastic, and the best types to get are those with a wide enough opening for you to put ice or energy drinks in. They are available in a variety of colors and shapes.

PUMPS

From full-size floor pumps to compact micro versions, mountain bike pumps come in a variety of shapes and sizes. A floor pump is useful to have at home or in the back of the car. It allows you to inflate the tires fully with minimum effort. A micro pump is good to take with you on the ride because it takes up little room.

BOTTLE CAGES

The best way to carry a bottle is on the frame in a bottle cage, where it will be easy to reach while you are going along. These cages will take bottles up to 1 liter (1.75 pint) capacity. It is advisable to get as stiff a cage as possible, which will hold the bottle securely. A bottle will fall out of some less-firm cages when you ride over bumps.

COMPUTERS

Bike computers are fun to have because they tell you exactly what you are doing. Most are waterproof and have seven functions: they tell you how far you have gone on one journey, what your total accumulated distance is, your maximum speed, your average speed, your cadence, the air temperature and the time.

Going to town

A mountain bike is designed to be perfect for riding off-road, but the wide wheels and powerful brakes, and the upright riding position that the bike gives you, are ideal for urban riding too. You may have to make a few adjustments and additions to your bike to make it legal and safer for riding on the road, but it is easy to change it back from a sleek road machine into its 'rock-eating' off-road form when you need to.

Rear light

Rear carrier

Rear mudguard

Toe clips and straps

ANTI-SCAM CAMS
Most mountain bikes have quick-release wheels which, unfortunately, are easy to steal. You can prevent your wheels from being stolen by fitting Anti-scam Cams. These gadgets will allow only you to take your wheels on and off, using a unique Allen key.

RACKS AND PANNIERS
If you are going to ride your bike to work or college you will probably need to carry a briefcase and possibly a change of clothing. A rack and panniers make a good way of carrying a heavy load. It is better than a backpack because you can balance the load safely, you will be able to carry far more, and you will not get a hot back.

LIGHTS
It is the law in most countries (and common sense) that when you are riding your bicycle on the road it has a reflector, and that you use front and rear lights after dark. There are many different types of lights available. Make sure that you get ones that meet the legal requirements.

Front light

Removable mudguard

Slick road tire

Anti-scam Cam

BELL

One of the main hazards of riding in towns and cities is pedestrians who may not take sufficient notice of cyclists when crossing the road. Ringing a loud bell is the ideal way to let someone know that you are coming.

MUDGUARD

To prevent you from getting covered in oil, water and mud that can spray up from the road, you should add mudguards. There are many varieties available and they are easy to detach when you want to turn your bike back into its off-road form.

TIRES

The heavy open tread of normal mountain bike tires will seriously slow you down on pavement, and can make cornering difficult. It is better to use road tires, and there are many types available for mountain bikes.

LOCKS

Mountain bikes are a popular theft target in all urban areas. Get the best possible lock you can afford, and use it every time you leave your bike unattended. It is worth spending up to 10 percent of the value of your bike on a lock, to guarantee getting one that is of good enough quality. You can buy brackets with which to attach U-locks, such as this one, to your bike while you are riding it.

Safety measures

Cycling in towns and cities is cheaper and often quicker than travelling by car or public transportation. You will have to share the road with other vehicles, breathe the polluted air, and thwart the thieves, but there are several things that you can do to make this less unpleasant. If you are properly prepared, and take the necessary care, you will find that urban riding can be a safe and enjoyable experience.

How to lock your bike

1 Find a strong post or railing to which to attach your bike. The post needs to be as wide as possible so that your lock fits snugly around it. This will make it difficult for a thief to get a crowbar through the lock to force it open.

2 Most mountain bikes come with a quick-release front wheel. This is easy for a thief to remove, so you must secure it. Remove the wheel and rest the bike down carefully on its fork.

3 Hold the front wheel next to the back wheel. Secure the bike to the post by putting your lock through both wheels and both chainstays, and around the post. Make sure that the lock goes around the rim and tire of each wheel, not just through the spokes.

4 Close the lock and check that it is firmly latched. Try to place the lock so that the keyhole is facing down. This may be more difficult for you to do but it will also make it difficult for someone else to pick the lock.

5 If you have a quick-release saddle and seat post, remove it and take it with you. If you do not, someone else might!

Safety clothing

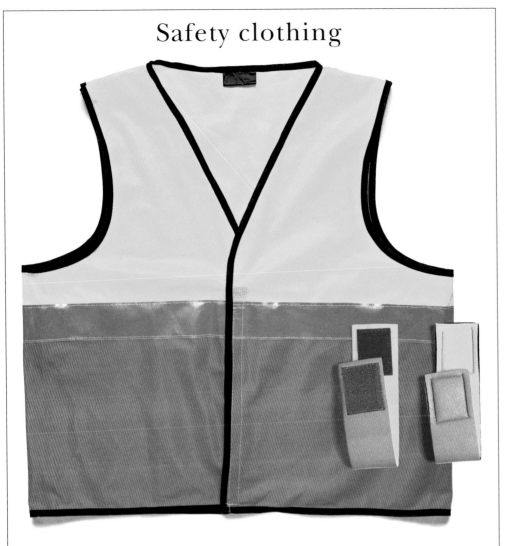

TROUSER CLIPS
When you ride in trousers, use clips to save your trousers from being snagged by the chain.

POLLUTION MASKS
You can wear a pollution mask to filter large particles of diesel, pollen and rust from the air. The best types to get are the ones with replaceable filters and blow out valves.

As a cyclist, it is very important that you can be seen. Car drivers may not always see a cyclist until the last minute, especially at night, so you should make yourself as noticeable as possible. One of the ways in which you can do this is by wearing a combination of reflective and fluorescent clothing, which will catch the eye of drivers. There is a wide range available, including vests, straps that go over the shoulder and ankle bands. The good thing about ankle bands is that they are especially noticeable because they move around with your legs as you pedal along.

Leaving your bike

DO NOT:
• Leave your bike locked up out of sight of a main street. A thief is less likely to be disturbed here.
• Leave your bike locked up somewhere other than at home overnight.
• Leave your bike unlocked outside a shop, even if you are just popping in for a second.

This is the most common time that a bike theft occurs.

DO:
• Try to put your bike in a lockable room at work.
• Inquire if there is a place where you can pay to leave your bike under a watchful eye.
• Lock your bike in your home when you go on vacation. Fix it to something immovable, such as a radiator, and cover it with a sheet so that passers-by will not immediately recognize it as a bike.
• Make anyone who borrows your bike fully aware of the need to lock it up, and show them how to do it properly.

INSURANCE
Insure your bike against theft and have third party insurance in case you ever cause an accident on your bike. The best way to get insurance is through a homeowner's policy or a special bike policy. Check the small print to make sure that your bike is covered in a variety of situations.

CHAPTER 4

Taking to the trail

The exhilaration you will experience when mountain biking comes from being able to combine riding a bike with being in beautiful surroundings. A mountain bike enables you to ride in many areas that are not accessible on other bikes, and to cover four times the distance that you would if you were hiking. There are, however, many things you must do to ensure that you will enjoy your ride, such as planning properly, remembering to take everything you need, and trying not to get lost. Hopefully you will never have to deal with an emergency but, before you set out, you should be confident in your ability to cope with anything.

Planning the ride

There are many different types of terrain and trails where you can ride a mountain bike, but do not set off aimlessly. Plan your route in advance taking into account how long it will take you, how hilly the terrain is and how skillful the people are who will be riding with you. If you are taking new riders with you, do not take them on your most difficult route, but take them somewhere that would be suitable for a novice.

SINGLETRACK
This type of trail—wide enough for only one bike—is great fun to ride on, but can be quite testing. Singletrack is often twisty and at some points you may not be able to see the trail very far ahead of you. Always be prepared to stop suddenly in case you meet another person or animal just around a corner.

DOUBLETRACK
Doubletrack is suitable for a family outing or for beginners, because it requires less technical ability, but it can still be fast and exhilarating. Be warned, there may be drainage ditches alongside, and it can be painful if you go off and crash into one.

MOUNTAIN BIKING CODE
- Give way to other trail users.
- Take all your rubbish home.
- Close gates after you.
- Never skid on wet soft ground (to avoid erosion).
- Ride with respect for your surroundings.
- Check that you have legal access before you ride.
- Do not ignore military 'keep-off' signs.

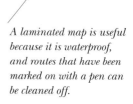
© Crown copyright

A laminated map is useful because it is waterproof, and routes that have been marked on with a pen can be cleaned off.

MAPPING THE ROUTE

Use a detailed map of the area where you are going. Anticipate how much you will have to ride up hills, because this will add a considerable amount of time to a ride. Choose a route that avoids boggy marshland, quarries and coastal paths which can be dangerous unless you know the area well or have an experienced guide.

Use a colored marker pen to mark your planned ride.

You will need a compass and pen for the ride.

DIRT ROAD

General-purpose dirt roads are usually accessible to a wide range of vehicles. They are normally well marked on maps and it is possible to plan long distance round trips by connecting lots together. Do be aware of other road users, such as jeeps and motorbikes.

LOGGING ROAD

Many big forests now have specific mountain bike trails going through them. You may require a permit to ride on some of these so check before you go. A disadvantage of these forest roads is that you can often come across heavy logging trucks or other forestry vehicles.

Tool kit

There is nothing worse than breaking down on a ride and having to walk home because you do not have the right equipment to fix your bike. Do not rely on other people to have what you need. Always take your own repair kit. You do not have to weigh yourself down with masses of heavy tools. Your kit can include just the few essential items that will enable you to repair most damage that you might incur on the trail.

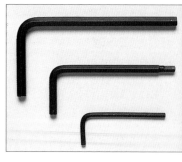

ALLEN KEYS

The Allen keys that you are most likely to need are 4 mm, 5 mm and 6 mm. Two other sizes which may be useful for longer journeys are 2 mm, for adjusting brakes, and 8 mm, for tightening some cranks that use this size. If possible get hardened Allen keys, which do not wear.

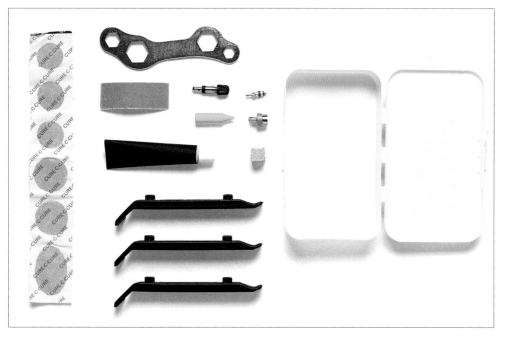

CHAIN RIVET EXTRACTOR

This is the only tool that you can use to repair a broken chain. It is absolutely vital. An individual one is far easier to use on the trail than one that is part of a multi-tool.

PUNCTURE REPAIR KIT

Take a puncture repair kit with you in case you have a run of bad luck and puncture both your inner tubes and your spare one. Most kits come with spare valves and a basic wrench, tire levers and patches. Try to get one that has nylon tire levers because they are difficult to break and will not damage the rim of your wheels. Make sure that the kit has sufficient patches and ones that are feather edged.

SPARE INNER TUBE AND SPOKES

A spare inner tube is the most likely thing you will need. Check that yours is the right size and that the valve fits your rims. A couple of spare spokes is always useful too. They are light and can be vital if you break one. A good way to carry them is to tape two together, put a small amount of Spoke Prep at one end and put them inside your handlebars.

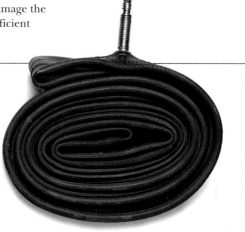

CRANK EXTRACTOR

This tool is important only if you are going on a long expedition far from anywhere. You will need one to remove your cranks if you need to repair a bent or loose chain-ring. Most crank extractors need to be tightened up with a 16 mm open-ended wrench.

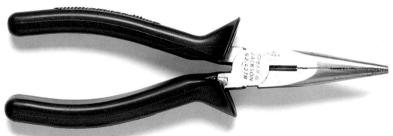

SMALL PLIERS

These can be used for a number of jobs that require good grip or are difficult with cold fingers – anything from pulling a thorn out of a tire to bending a damaged chain link.

BOX-END WRENCH

There are many jobs on a bike for which a box-end wrench is useful, especially when a large amount of leverage is not required. You can also fit one over an Allen key to increase leverage.

MULTI-TOOL

This is like a penknife, with a selection of tools fitted into one. Good ones are made by companies such as Minora, Cannondale and Park Tools. Most will have 2 mm, 4 mm, 5 mm, and 6 mm Allen keys, and Phillips and regular flat screwdrivers. The advantage of a multi-tool is that it keeps the tools in one place.

CHAINRING BOLT

It is always worth carrying a spare one.

PUMP

Your pump must be reliable and efficient – imagine changing a flat in the worst possible conditions – so do not get a cheap one. There are many compact pumps with a double action which are easy to carry and use.

RACING TOOL KIT

If you are going to race, you need to carry only the things that you could use to make a quick repair. If you break something really major, you will probably have to pull out of the race. The essential things for a racing tool kit are a spare inner tube, a pair of tire levers, a Ritchey CPR (compact racing) tool and a pump, or CO_2 cartridge if you know how to use one.

Ritchey CPR tool

ZIP TIES AND TOE STRAPS

Zip ties are strong and can be used to hold things on your bike that have come off. Toe straps can be used for larger things in the same way, such as for tying a water bottle to the frame to stop it from bouncing out when you go over rocky terrain.

SPARE CHAIN LINKS

If you have room take a small section of chain that matches the one on your bike. If you snap your chain badly, the broken links will probably be too damaged to rejoin. You will then have to remove the damaged links and insert some new ones. Remember that some Shimano IG and HG chains rely on special joining links which you may need as well.

Your pack

It is important to be fully prepared for your ride. As well as ensuring that your bike is in full working order, and that you have everything you need for it, you must check that you have everything you need for yourself. This is especially important if you are planning to ride a long way and may go far away from civilization. You can put yourself in unnecessary danger if you do not take the essential things. You are bound to need something just when you haven't got it.

Off-road trails

Providing you prepare properly and take the right things, you should have no problems on a general off-road ride. It is very important that you have enough to eat and drink. You use a huge amount of energy when riding a bike, and must replenish this as you go, especially on a long-distance ride. Wear clothing that is suitable for the time of year and climate, and enjoy yourself.

BEFORE YOU GO
• Check with people with whom you have not ridden before to establish what their riding capabilities are, and discuss any proposed routes to see that everyone is up to them.
• Check that you can complete your planned route in the daylight hours available, with time to spare.
• Check the weather forecast before you set out and change your plans if necessary.

ESSENTIAL ITEMS TO CARRY
• Sunscreen: It is easy to get sunburnt when riding a bike since you may not be aware of the temperature because you will be cooled by the breeze.
• Insect repellent: When you sweat you attract more insects.
• Antihistamine: This provides relief from insect bites and stings, and from rashes caused by poisonous plants.
• Money: You should take enough money to cover planned and emergency expenses, such as getting home by public transportation, and sufficient change for a phone call in case of an emergency.

FOOD AND DRINK TO TAKE
• Bananas: These are high in carbohydrates and energy, contain potassium which stops you from getting cramps, and are easily digestible.
• Dried fruit: This is an excellent source of energy; it is light and easy to carry.
• Energy bars: There are many different energy bars on the market that contain a high level of carbohydrates and instant energy.
• Water: Cool water is absorbed faster than any other liquid. On a long ride, you should drink water every 20 to 30 minutes to prevent your body from dehydrating. Never drink water from a stream unless you know it is close to a good spring.
• Energy drinks: These replace minerals, salts and carbohydrates, but are not as rapidly absorbed into the bloodstream as water.

Dried apricots

Nuts

CLOTHES TO WEAR
• Helmet: Always wear a helmet because if you crash and hit your head it could be fatal without one.
• Gloves: Always wear gloves for comfort on a long ride, and to protect your hands if you crash.
• Jacket: A lightweight windproof jacket will keep you warm if you have to stop in a windy spot. There are many that pack down very small and can be carried easily.
• Layers of clothing: Wearing several thin layers is the best way of keeping warm in cool weather. You can also adjust your temperature throughout the day by taking different layers off or putting them on.

Bananas

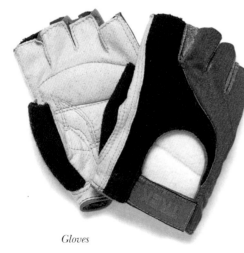

Gloves

In the mountains

When you are going riding in the mountains, always prepare for the worst. Take the same things with you as you would on an ordinary off-road ride, plus some extra items to cater to the more difficult conditions. Do not ride on your own and always make sure that you have suitable clothing that will keep you warm and therefore in a good state of mind.

BEFORE YOU GO

• Check the weather forecast and do not set out if you are at all unsure. Remember, weather conditions are prone to change very quickly in the mountains.
• Make sure that someone else knows where you are riding and what time to expect you back.
• Do not let your ego get in the way of your judgment and persuade you to plan a ride that is beyond your ability or that of anyone in your party.

Rear light

Front light

CLOTHES TO TAKE

• Gore-tex gloves and socks These are expensive, but the best things to keep your hands and feet snug and dry.
• Balaclava: It is very important to reduce heat loss through your head. A balaclava is the headgear that does this best and it goes under a helmet.
• Quick-drying clothes: Do not wear clothing that will hold water and not dry quickly. Wind-chill can bring your body temperature down very quickly if you are wearing wet clothing, and this can lead to hypothermia.
• Extra clothing: Always carry an extra layer of clothing in case you are involved in an accident and need to keep that little bit warmer.
• Mountaineering clothing: Consider wearing this when you need the best protection in extreme conditions.

EMERGENCY EQUIPMENT TO CARRY

• Survival blanket or bag: Take this in case someone is injured and needs to be left while you find help.
• Whistle: If you get lost in fog or in the dark you can blow this to help people find you.
• Red LED light: A good-quality light can be seen up to 2.5 miles away and one that flashes is very noticeable.
• Halogen front light or mag-light-type flashlight: If you get stuck in the dark, a good-quality flashlight is essential to help you find your way back or signal for help.
• High-energy food: This will keep you going when you are feeling down. Avoid ones with a high sugar content because they tend to raise your blood sugar level very high, which then drops again quickly.
• Thermos of hot drink: This will keep your body temperature high and is good for morale. Coffee is best because it will help you to stay awake which can make a difference between life and death.
• Compass and map: Make sure that you know how to use these. They are essential so that you can find out where you are.
• First-aid kit: A basic kit incorporating Band-Aids, gauze pads, adhesive tape and pain killers is necessary in case of an accident.
• Swiss army knife and matches: These can be useful in many situations.

Dates

Raisins

Energy bars

Compass

Pre-ride checks

Before you go on a ride, check that your bike is in full working order. It is frustrating if your bike breaks down, especially if the breakdown could have been avoided. It is also annoying for any other people riding with you, if they have to wait for you to make repairs. A few easy checks, which will take you only a matter of minutes, may save you from a long walk home and a wasted day.

BRAKE TENSION
Pull your brakes hard to see that you have sufficient tension on the cable. The brake blocks should come into contact with the rim before the lever hits the handlebar.

BRAKE PADS
Release the straddle wire to look at the brake blocks. Check that they are not too worn. It is important that you have not worn through to the metal at the base.

BRAKE CABLES
Check that none of the cables are frayed. This could be catastrophic because the cables will break when you put the most pressure on them – when you need them most.

DERAILLEURS
Run the bike through the gears to check that your derailleurs are set up properly, and also to check gear cable tension. You will not be able to change gear smoothly if these are not correct.

CHAIN
Check that your chain does not have any stiff or damaged links in it. A good way to tell is by spinning the cranks backwards. If a link is damaged it will cause the chain to jump on the sprockets.

HEADSET
Check before a ride that your headset is not loose. A loose headset is incredibly irritating and will damage the bike if you ride with one. It can be tightened with the correct spanner.

SHOP SERVICE
Most bike shops will check your bike over for a small charge. It is a good idea to get to know your bike, even if you do not want to work on it yourself. At least you will know what is wrong if it does need repairs.

HANDLEBARS
Make sure that the bolt that clamps the stem to the handlebars is tight. It is dangerous to ride with it loose. It can be tightened with either a 5 or 6 mm Allen key.

STEM
Check that your stem bolt is tight in the frame. If it is loose, the handlebars can move in a different direction from the front wheel. Tighten it with a 6 mm Allen key.

SADDLE AND SEAT POST
Check that the height of your saddle is correct and that the clamp is bolted tightly. If you ride while the clamp is loose, you can damage the calibrations on the seat post.

FINAL CHECK
Once you have completed all of these checks, take your bike out for a quick spin around the block. Listen and feel for anything that doesn't seem right. Go up and down through all the gears, checking that they work properly, and give the brakes a hard test.

TIRE PRESSURE
Check that both your tires are properly inflated. If you do not have a tire pressure gauge, squeeze the sides of the tire. They should just give.

SIDEWALL
Check the sidewalls of the tires to make sure that the brake blocks have not damaged them. If they are weakened, you could have a blowout, which can be dangerous.

TIRE CARCASS
Check that the carcass of the tire isn't damaged. A worn tire is far more prone to puncturing than a new one. (The tire shown here is an extreme case.)

WHEELS
Spin the wheels to check that they are straight, using the brake blocks as a guide. Listen for a scuffing noise, which will be the rim hitting the brake block, indicating a dent in the rim.

SPOKES
Check that the spokes are at the right tension and are not damaged. Do not adjust spokes unless you are confident about what you are doing. If in doubt seek help from a bike shop.

Getting there

In order to sample new mountain-biking terrain, you may have to travel some distance away from where you live. If you cannot, or do not want to ride to your destination, you will have to find a means of transporting your bike. Even without a car this should not be a problem in most countries. As long as you pack the bike up carefully, you will be able to take it on public transportation with little risk of damaging it.

TRAIN

Going by train is an easy way to get yourself and your bike to where you want to ride. There are many different regional and national policies on taking a bike on a train, so always find out what the relevant one is before planning a ride around a particular network. Remember to lock the bike up securely before leaving it unattended anywhere on a train.

AIRPLANE

Most major airlines will be happy to carry your bike to your destination, but check before you buy a ticket. To carry your bike on a plane it will need to be packed in a bike bag or box. Assemble your bike as soon as you can after you arrive, in case something is damaged and you need to claim on your insurance.

BUS

Taking a bike on a bus may prove more difficult, because of the lack of room. Some companies may allow you to take a bike if it is bagged up and can be treated as a large suitcase. Check in advance so that you don't get stranded.

BAGGING A BIKE

1 Remove the wheels and their skewers and let the tires down. Undo the handlebar stem with a 6 mm Allen key and pull it out of the forks. Unscrew the pedals with a 15 mm wrench then remove the seat post and saddle.

2 Put the wheel covers on, then put the wheels in the bag. Lay the bike down in the bag on its side and rotate the forks towards the rear of the bike. Position the handlebars between the top tube and down tube, packing them well with bubble wrap or cardboard. Put the pedals and wheel skewers into the bag supplied, and lay this over the chain and rear derailleur.

3 Check that you have put everything in the bag that you took off the bike, and have packed all the tools that you will need to put the bike back together. Zip up the bag and tighten it using the tensioners on the outside, to prevent the bike parts from moving about inside the bag if it is thrown around on the journey.

70

TRUNK-RACKS

One of the best ways to transport your bike by car is on a trunk-rack, and 99 percent of cars can be fitted with one. Most racks will take up to three bikes, but be sure to get one that is sturdy enough. When you have bikes on the back of your car, make sure that your lights and number plate can still be seen.

TOW-BAR RACKS

These are racks that are specifically designed to fit on tow-bars. These are normally just as secure as trunk-racks. Some allow you to use your tow-bar for towing at the same time.

TOW-PLATES

It is dangerous and illegal to cover up your rear lights so that they cannot be seen by other road users. If you cannot avoid this, use a tow-plate. This has space for a license plate, and lights which you connect to the car's lights.

ROOF-RACKS

The advantages of a roof-rack are that it will not obscure your rearview vision and you can carry more weight on one. The disadvantages are that your car will consume more fuel, due to the poor aerodynamics, and it can be awkward lifting a bike on after a tiring ride. Many roof-racks have fittings that you can change to carry anything from bikes to skis to canoes.

On the trail

When out riding your mountain bike, you must remember that you are a representative of your sport. In order for trails to remain open for mountain biking, and for more trails to be made available, it is important that you present the right image. Other people use the trails and they have a right to enjoy them too. Always be considerate, friendly and helpful and think of everyone's safety on the trail including your own.

EMERGENCIES

You can reduce the chance of serious injury by always wearing a helmet and not taking unnecessary risks when riding. But due to the nature of off-road riding it is quite possible that you will be involved in an accident at some stage. It is a good idea to learn some basic first aid so that you know what to do if a companion is injured. If you are injured yourself, get help, which is one reason why you should always try to ride with someone else.

DEALING WITH AN INJURED PERSON

If the person is unconscious, put him on his side in the recovery position while you go to get help. If you think the person may have sustained a head injury do not remove his helmet, but make sure that the strap is not restricting breathing. Put something over him to keep him warm. If the person is conscious, find out how serious the injury is, then get help if necessary. Make the casualty as warm and comfortable as possible. If you have to leave an injured person on his own, make sure that you will be able to find him again by using a piece of bright clothing as a marker, held down by a stone or attached to a tree.

DOGS

Some dogs that you meet on a trail may chase you. It can be better to stop until the dog goes out of sight. If passing an unaccompanied dog from behind, build up sufficient speed to carry you past the dog before it gets time to think. If a dog does go for you, use your pump to fend it off.

HORSES

Sudden movements and noises are likely to startle a horse, and this can be dangerous for you as well as for the rider. When you meet a horse coming in the oppostite direction, stop to one side and allow the horse to pass. Wait for it to get well away before you set off again. If approaching a horse from behind, carefully warn the rider that you are there. She may stop to allow you to go on but, if not, wait until there is plenty of room before attempting to pass.

WALKERS

When you see a walker on the trail, slow down immediately. If you are going in opposite directions, pull to one side and allow the walker to pass, giving him a friendly greeting. If you are approaching from behind, let him know you are there. Remember, a bike can be quite silent. Pass only when there is room to do so and, again, give a friendly greeting and thank the walker if he stands aside for you.

Do not come up suddenly behind people and push past, forcing them off the track. They have as much right to be there as you do. Never ride past people at speed without consideration. This type of aggressive riding will lead only to complaints and may lead to trails being closed to mountain bikers.

The right way

...and the wrong way.

Finding the way

Mountain biking, by its very nature, can lead to your getting lost. The combination of tight twisting trails and changes in scenery can easily disorient you. Learn to read a map and use a compass so that you can figure out where you are and which way to go. It is a good idea to leave a map of your proposed route at home so that someone will know where to look for you if you don't come home.

STAYING ON TRACK

Always carry a map of the area where you are riding, and a compass. Mark on the map the point at which you start and where you intend to get to. Stop every so often to check that you are going the right way. Look for distinctive features shown on the map, such as rivers, forested areas, trails and steep hills to figure out where you are. Use your compass to find out which direction you are facing.

FINDING A BEARING

A compass bearing becomes essential once you are lost and is always useful in forestry areas. The following steps will help you determine the direction to travel according to the route on your map.

1 Roughly orient the map so that the north edge is facing north.

2 Place the compass flat on the map with the edge of its baseplate aligned along the direction of travel. In other words, in line with where you are currently standing and the next point on the route.

3 Rotate the compass bezel until the N on the compass dial points to North on the map. You have now taken the bearing.

4 Take the compass off the map and turn yourself around until the red end of the needle points to N on the compass dial. The large 'direction of travel' arrow will now point precisely at your destination.

5 Choose a landmark along this line and ride towards it. When you reach the landmark, repeat the procedure until you reach your destination.

HOW LONG WILL IT TAKE?

Keep an eye on the time as you ride. By using your bicycle computer and watch, you can calculate how long it will take you to cycle to your destination. Start your trip with your computer at zero. After an hour, check the distance that you have covered and you will know what your approximate speed is. Figure out how far you have to go and then how long it will take you, adding on extra time for any long climbs you know you will have.

IF YOU GET LOST

Don't panic. Stay in a group and work together to find your way home. Don't separate: both parties may end up lost! Retrace your steps to a point where you know where you are. If necessary go back to the start the way you came. Try to rejoin the route at a later stage, or find a road alternative on the map. If you can't do this, stop at the next sign or landmark, consult your map and take a compass bearing.

On-trail repairs

While out riding, you may have a mechanical problem which, in order to get home, you will have to fix on the trail. There will be certain times when you don't have the correct tools or part to fix your bike, but there are many ways of doing an emergency repair to avoid a long walk home. These makeshift repairs will not last forever, but they will probably allow you to ride home.

No inner tube

If your inner tube is damaged beyond repair, and you don't have a spare one, remove the inner tube and tightly pack the tire with grass. Do not ride on a flat tire because you will damage it and the rim of the wheel.

Split inner tube

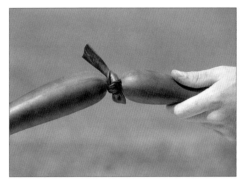

If your tire has had a major blowout, and the inner tube is severely split, it is probably impossible to repair. If so, try cutting the tube at the split and tying the two ends in a tight knot. Pump the tire up as high as you can.

Emergency crank tightening

If you try to ride your bike with a loose crank, you risk wearing it out and it falling off. A crude but effective way of tightening it up is to hit it with a piece of wood or a rock.

Changing an inner tube

1 Release your brakes before you try to take the wheel off, otherwise you will have trouble getting the wheel out.

2 Remove the wheel from the bike. The majority of mountain bikes have quick-release wheels, making this fairly straightforward.

3 Use a tire lever to pry the tire off the wheel all the way around. Run your hand around inside the tire to find what caused the puncture and remove it.

4 Slightly inflate the new inner tube. This will help to prevent it from being caught between the tire beading and the rim.

5 Put the tire back around the wheel, insert the valve of the inner tube, then tuck the tube into the tire, making sure that it is not pinched between the tire and the rim.

6 Pump up the tire, checking that it is seated properly and not bulging off the rim anywhere, because this can cause a blowout. Reinflate it to the pressure stated on the tire.

Patching an inner tube

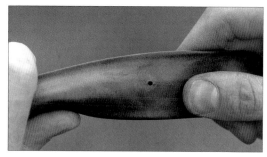

1 If you get a puncture and do not have a spare inner tube, patch the old one. Find the hole by inflating the tube, then running it past your lips to feel for air coming out.

2 Once you have felt the air, look for the hole so that you know exactly where to put the patch. It is a good idea to mark the hole in some way so that you do not lose it.

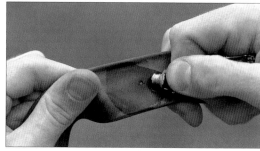

3 Rub the area around the hole with a piece of sandpaper so that the glue for the patch will have a rough surface to adhere to.

4 Put a small amount of glue around the hole. Do not put too much on. Spread it evenly with your finger then allow it to dry for about five minutes.

5 Remove the patch from the foil packing, but leave on the cellophane. Put the patch in position over the hole then remove excess glue by pushing outwards from the center.

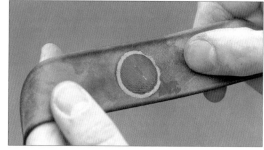

JOINING A BROKEN CHAIN

In most cases, you can rejoin a broken chain only if you have a chain tool. (It is important that you use the correct chain tool for your chain.) If possible, replace the damaged chain links with some new ones.

6 Leave the patch for about five minutes for the glue to dry. Remove the cellophane covering and check that the patch is well attached before putting the tube back into the tire.

Repairing a trashed rear derailleur

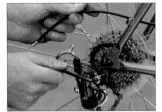

1 If you catch your rear derailleur on an obstacle it will probably become jammed up and break. It has such a complex mechanism that it will not function if badly damaged and it is best to remove it altogether.

2 Undo the gear cable and unscrew the rear derailleur from the frame with a 5 mm Allen key. Tuck the gear cable up around the frame and underneath the saddle to prevent it from catching in the wheel. Then break the chain using a chain link extractor.

3 Route the chain on the middle chainring and the middle rear sprocket. In this gear you will probably be able to ride most of the way home. You will have to shorten the chain so find the correct length and remove the necessary number of links.

4 Rejoin the chain off the bike then put it on the middle rear sprocket and on the top of the middle chain-ring. Move the pedals around to check that the chain is the correct length. If it is too long it will jump.

Straightening a badly buckled wheel

2 Find a large flat stone and lay the wheel over it so that the wheel axle rests against the stone. Stand with one foot on the side of the wheel resting on the ground, and your other foot on the point of the wheel that is most buckled.

Working on a bike can be dirty work. The best thing to use to remove grease, oil and dirt from your hands after carrying out on-trail repairs is grass. Simply grab a handful of grass and rub it between your hands.

1 If you have a major crash or land heavily from a jump, you could buckle your wheel. You will not be able to ride the bike on a buckled wheel because the wheel will not spin around without hitting the forks and the frame. You must therefore remove the wheel and straighten it.

3 Using all your body weight press down hard with your top foot to straighten the wheel. If it is still slightly buckled, release the tension on your brakes until the tire does not rub against the brake blocks.

When you get home

After your ride, clean and lubricate your bike as soon as possible. It is better for the bike if it is cleaned when mud is still wet. Use lots of hot, soapy water and a soft brush. Avoid using a high-pressure hose because this can damage your sealed bearings. Lubricate all the moving parts to keep them running smoothly and to help prevent them from corroding. If you look after your bike the parts will last much longer.

Cleaning

1 Use dish washing liquid or car shampoo in half a bucket of warm water. Starting from the top, wash the whole bike. Use a generous amount to avoid scratching the paintwork.

2 A small brush is especially useful for cleaning out tight spaces where mud can collect. Thoroughly clean wheel rims and brake blocks as dirty rims give less grip in braking.

3 Use degreaser to remove caked-on dirt and oil residues. Let the degreaser soak in and then attack with an old toothbrush. Clean sprockets and chain will give a very smooth run.

4 After special attention has been paid to brakes, rims, sprockets, chain, derailleurs and cable housings, then rinse off. Use a sponge to cascade water over the bike.

5 Wipe down the frame with a chamois leather or clean towel and leave it to stand to dry off completely. Squirt spray lube over bare metal parts to displace the water and prevent rust.

Lubricating

1 Lubricate the brake lever pivots. Squeeze the lever a couple of times to work the lubricant in.

2 Lubricate the pivots on both front and rear brakes. Wipe off any oil that gets on the rim or brake blocks.

3 Lubricate cables where they go through the frame or into the brake levers or gear shifters.

4 Lubricate the front and rear derailleur pivots and the pulley wheels on the rear derailleur.

5 Use a heavier mineral oil on the chain. Don't use a vegetable based oil as this leaves a sticky residue.

RUST PREVENTION

After washing your bike, turn it upside down to allow any water that has got inside the frame to drain out. Then use a spray lubricant to spray through the ventilation holes on the frame. This will prevent the frame from rusting inside which can be catastrophic.

CHAPTER 5

Riding techniques

Riding your mountain bike off-road will involve negotiating many different surfaces, inclines, and obstacles. You may find a fallen tree across the trail or suddenly arrive at the top of a near-vertical slope. There are techniques for dealing with different obstacles, but do not feel that you have to stay on your bike at all times. There will be occasions when it is much better to get off and carry your bike. As you improve your riding technique you will gradually build up confidence until you are able to tackle most things you come across.

Getting fit

In order to be able to enjoy a long day's ride over varying terrain, it is important to be reasonably fit. If you are just starting out, don't be put off. Most people have a reasonable level of fitness and the best way to get fit for cycling is by cycling. Ride your bike regularly and, with a small amount of training and practice, you will gradually improve until you will be able to keep up with more experienced riders.

KEEPING TRACK

Keep a diary of the training you do and targets you reach. This is a good way of measuring your fitness improvements. Set yourself a date by when you want to get fit and set different goals up to this time. Do not rush it.

CYCLING

Climbing hills on a bike is also good for getting fit. If you stay in the saddle it will improve your power. Try to stay in one gear and you will find that you have to work hard to maintain your speed and to keep your rpm up. Climbing out of the saddle will improve your upper body fitness because you use your body weight, arms and shoulders to help propel the bike forwards.

RUNNING

One way to train is to run uphill. This will increase your stamina and strength and will improve your recovery time. You may find this hard work to begin with but it is well worth the effort.

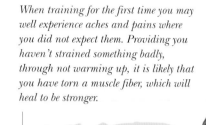

FIT TO RIDE

Don't try to get fit overnight. It will take time, but don't let this put you off. Once you are fit, you will find you are able to go farther and longer without getting tired, and will enjoy your rides more.

TRAINING EFFICIENTLY

If you are serious about getting fit, a heart rate monitor is a useful tool. Your heartbeat gives the best indication of your level of exertion. To work out the maximum rate at which your heart can beat, take your age away from 220. Do not exceed this rate. The most efficient way to train is at 80 percent of your maximum.

When training for the first time you may well experience aches and pains where you did not expect them. Providing you haven't strained something badly, through not warming up, it is likely that you have torn a muscle fiber, which will heal to be stronger.

You may suffer a burning sensation in the back of your calves while climbing. This is normally caused by the build-up of lactic acid. As your fitness increases, your body's ability to deal with lactic acid will improve.

Toe clips and straps will greatly enhance your pedalling efficiency, helping you to get fitter.

Warming up

Get into the habit of stretching before going for a ride, then you are far less likely to get an injury. While you cycle, some parts of your body are static while others are moving. This can cause certain muscles to get tired quickly, such as those in your neck. By doing simple stretches you will greatly improve your flexibility and endurance.

BACK

Do not do this if you don't feel comfortable. Sit down on the floor with your legs stretched out in front of you and gradually lean forwards. Try to curl your back down from the waist and extend forward slowly. Hold the stretch for 30 seconds.

SIT UPS

Sit ups are not a stretch as such, but this simple exercise can help in several ways. First it will help you to strengthen your lower back which will improve comfort on long rides.

It will also help strengthen your stomach which, together with lower back muscles, helps support your internal organs. These get shaken around when riding on very bumpy ground and the result can be painful. This internal shake-up can be mistaken for backache.

When doing sit ups, put your hands by the side of your head, keep both feet firmly on the ground and raise your torso at a controlled speed. When you are in the upright position, begin to lower your back down slowly. To do this correctly is far more beneficial than doing 50 as fast as you can. Start by doing 20 and work up gradually.

NECK

It is important to stretch your neck because your head is heavy and you do not want to risk damaging your neck. Stand relaxed and turn your head from left to right slowly, holding it for at least 30 seconds at the farthest reach on each side. Also, gently lift and tuck in your chin.

CALVES AND HAMSTRINGS

This is a good way of stretching your calves and hamstrings gently. Stand on a step with one foot fully on and the ball of other foot on the edge of the step. Shift your weight gradually to the foot that is partly on the step and press down gradually. You will feel the muscles stretch. Do the same on the other leg.

Cross training

CALVES
If you stretch your calves you are less likely to get cramps. Push against a wall, with one leg extended behind, and push back with your thigh for 30 seconds. Then move your foot farther back and hold this for 30 seconds. Do the same with the other leg.

QUADS
Stand on one leg and bend the other leg up in front of you. Clasp your hands together around this leg and pull it up to your chest, keeping your back straight. Hold this position for approximately 30 seconds and then do the same with the other leg.

RUNNING
A quick way to build up your fitness is by running. This uses muscles similar to those used in cycling, and is good for building up stamina.

IN-LINE SKATING
In-line skating is good for building up power in your thighs, which are used on a bike for bursts of explosive sprinting. Skating develops coordination, which you need on a bike.

HAMSTRINGS
Stand up and cross one leg in front of the other and keep your feet together. Gently bend forwards letting your upper body extend down. Hold this position for 30 seconds, then do the same crossing the other leg in front.

SHOULDERS
Join your fingers behind you by reaching one hand over your shoulder and the other up behind. Point your upper elbow straight upwards and hold this position for 30 seconds. Do the same on the opposite side.

WINTER TRAINING
Use a weight machine when you are not riding regularly. This will exercise the muscles in your lower back, and will help to maintain the strength of your upper body, which is important for sprinting and descending.

The riding position

When you are riding your bike, you must feel comfortable so that you can keep going for long distances and enjoy it. Make sure that your bike is set up in the best possible way for you. Your riding position should also be the most efficient one. If it is not, you will be more tired than you need be at the end of the day. When you first start riding, make a point of checking as you go along that you are riding properly. You will soon fall into the position naturally, the moment you get on the bike.

Keep your weight over both wheels to maintain traction.

Lower your seat approximately ½ inch when going over very bumpy ground, because the bike will move up and down a fair amount beneath you.

CORRECT POSITION
The ideal riding position for off-road riding on the flat is with your weight spread equally over both the wheels. Bend at the hip and keep your back fairly flat. Your arms should be relaxed and your head up in a comfortable position. You need to be able to see where you are going without getting neck ache.

The most efficient position for your foot is with the center of the ball of your foot over the pedal axle.

Keep your head up so that you can see what is ahead.

Your arms must not be too stretched out.

The handlebars should be 2 to 4 inches lower than the saddle.

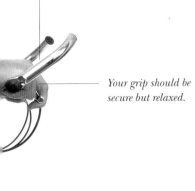

Your grip should be secure but relaxed.

CLIMBING

When you are climbing a hill, slide forwards on the saddle and sink your weight low over the bike to help maintain traction. Avoid standing up as this could make the wheels spin. Push your elbows down and keep your head up so that you can see where you are going. Do not tense up. If you stay relaxed you will be able to adjust for changes in the terrain without losing traction of the wheels.

SPRINTING

When sprinting, you want to combine your body weight and acceleration to drive the pedals forwards. Keep your weight balanced over both wheels. If you put too much weight over the front of the bike, the back wheel will lose traction. Also, if your gears were to slip, you could lose balance and crash. Try not to push the bike from side to side beneath you. You will lose speed and will make the bike unstable.

DESCENDING

On fast descents, always make sure you are in control of the bike. Keep your hands over the brakes in a light but firm grip and the elbows relaxed rather than locked so as to absorb the bumps. Keep your eyes up, look ahead and pick your line. Your weight should be down and towards the back of the bike. This is vital on steep slopes when you will have to push your weight right off the back of the saddle.

Braking and shifting

The correct use of the gears and brakes on a mountain bike is essential for a safe ride. The brakes are extremely powerful and should be used with caution until you get used to them, otherwise you will go straight over the handlebars. And if you select the wrong gear in the middle of a climb, you could come to an abrupt halt. Not only will you probably fall off but you will have to walk up the hill. Master these controls to help you ride through any technical section of a trail that you encounter.

FRONT BRAKE
The front brake is very powerful, as demonstrated here with this trick, which is very easy to do by simply pulling on the front brake and pushing your weight slightly forward. Unfortunately it can be even easier to jam on the front brake and go over the handlebars. So be careful, especially on descents, and practise mastering use of the front brake.

Left-hand shifter controls the front derailleur.

SHIFTING GEAR
When shifting gear, never look down to see which gear you are in. Always look where you are going. You just need to be in the gear that feels best at the time. It doesn't really matter which one it is. Anticipate the next gear shift and change in good time.

Emergency braking

1 If you are speeding down a hill and turn a corner to see an obstacle on the trail that you know you will not be able to get over or past, you will have to do an emergency stop.

2 Get as low and as far back on the bike as possible so that your stomach is almost on the saddle. Pull your front brake smoothly, gradually increasing pressure. Do not jam it on suddenly because you are likely to go over the handlebars.

3 Keep the bike pointing forwards to prevent the front wheel from skidding away. You may feel the back wheel come off the ground because of the pull on the front brake. It will go down if you keep your weight down and back.

4 You should come to a safe standstill without crashing into the obstacle. Remember that braking in the wet is more difficult. It takes longer to stop and you risk skidding if you brake going around a corner. Take things more slowly so you do not risk having to do an emergency stop. And do not assume that you know what is around a familiar corner. Trail conditions can change from one week to the next.

Right-hand shifter controls the rear derailleur.

Brake levers should be within easy reach.

Eight-speed X-ray Grip Shift.

BRAKING
The best way to brake is by feathering (pulling the brakes on and off). This reduces your speed rapidly and you are less likely to skid.

Cornering

There are certain basic rules that apply to all cornering techniques. These are: always extend and weight your outside leg when leaning into a corner; always keep focused on the farthest point of the corner as you turn; always brake before the corner and not while going through it. Apply these rules to all corners and you should not have any problems.

STEEP TRAVERSE
You may occasionally have to traverse an off-camber surface. In this situation apply the main rules of turning – keep your speed controlled and put your weight on your outside foot. Concentrate on keeping as high a line as possible across the traverse by turning into it.

Low-speed turn

1 When riding on technical singletrack, keep a loose grip so that you will be able to make any sudden changes of direction. When you come to a corner, brake before you go into it to control your speed. Do not brake on the corner.

2 Look ahead as far as possible and try to pick the smoothest line to ride through the corner. On a low-speed turn, it is not necessary to take the tightest, fastest line. It is more important that you follow a smooth curve.

3 Watch out for anything on the ground, such as a wet tree root or large stone, which could cause you to skid or bounce off the trail. If you see it in time you will be able to miss it and thus avoid an accident.

4 Change down a gear before exiting the corner. Then you will be able to accelerate out of the corner and regain your pace as soon as possible. Take up the correct position again and continue on down the hill.

High-speed turn

1 If you are going very fast and come to a corner, try to cut your speed before entering the corner by feathering the brakes.

2 Take the widest possible line as you enter the corner. This will give you more room to turn. Keep your outside leg extended.

3 Once you are in the corner, aim as close as possible to the center of the apex. As you turn, remember to keep all your weight pushing hard down on your outside foot. This will prevent you from losing traction.

4 Lean as much as possible into the corner. On no account pull the brakes while you are cornering, even if you think you are going too fast. You will just lose control.

5 When you have negotiated the corner, stand out of the saddle and pedal hard to pick up your speed. Be prepared to slow down if there is something or someone on the trail.

Climbing

The hills that you will climb on a mountain bike are likely to be much steeper, and definitely rougher, than those you might climb on a conventional bike. If you are equipped with proper off-road tires and enough gears, these tips will help you ride up hills – and make it to the top.

PRACTICING
Don't expect always to get up a serious technical climb the first time. It is difficult to find the best line up a slope when you are concentrating on simply getting up. With practice you will learn how to choose the line and enjoy the climb.

1 Before climbing a hill, select the right gear. You will find it very difficult to make a smooth gear change when hauling up a steep slope. It is much easier to keep climbing smoothly if you change gear before you need to.

2 Remain in the saddle to keep weight on your wheels, which will give you better traction. Slide forwards on the saddle and keep your body low by dropping your elbows and head. This keeps your weight low.

3 As you climb, maintain your momentum so that if you hit a small bump you will be carried over it rather than brought to a halt. The best way to keep your momentum going is to spin the pedals quickly.

4 If you encounter a very technical section on the climb, you may have to stand up out of the saddle to get the bike through the section. Do not put all your body weight into your pedalling because this can result in the back wheel spinning out. Coax the bike over the object instead of trying to obliterate it.

KEEPING TO THE BEST LINE

It is important to remember always to look ahead when climbing, to find the best possible route avoiding patches of loose rocks and deep ruts. Keep your grip on the handlebars quite loose so that if you have to make small steering adjustments as you go over obstacles you will not lose your line.

Keep your body weight low to maintain better traction.

The knobbier the tire tread, the better the traction you will have for climbing.

MORE TRACTION

If you find that you are always losing traction on a climb, you may have your tires pumped up too high. If you let the tires down a fraction you will put more tread in contact with the ground. This will give you much better traction.

Descending

One of the most exhilarating parts of mountain biking is the downhill. It can also be one of the most frightening if you are out of control, because you are likely to crash. All you need to be able to do to negotiate any hill safely is to take up the correct riding position, know when to brake, and pick the best line. Start on a gentle slope then gradually tackle steeper slopes as you build up your confidence and skill.

LOWER YOUR SADDLE

Most mountain bikes have a quick-release lever on the seat post. This is designed to let you lower your saddle for going down steep hills. You can then get farther back off the saddle when you are descending. This will improve your confidence and technique.

CORRECT POSITION

One of the most important things to do when going down a steep hill is to push your weight well back over the back wheel. This lowers your center of gravity and will help to stop you from going over the handlbars should the bike stop suddenly.

1 As you approach the hill, make sure that you are in control of your speed. Feather your front brake to reduce your speed without locking up your brakes.

2 Stand up on the pedals and move backwards behind the saddle so that your weight is well over the back wheel. Keep two fingers on each brake lever so that you remain in control.

3 On bumpy ground, put your bike into gear with the chain on the large chainring and one of the middle sprockets at the back. This will reduce the chance of your chain falling off.

4 It is important to use your legs and arms as a form of suspension for your body. Keep the pedals level so that you are poised on the bike. Do not grip the handlebars too tightly because this can cause your hands to cramp up, resulting in a major loss of control. This is referred to as a 'deathgrip.'

FREE FEET
At the top of any steep hill you should loosen your toe straps. You will then be able to separate easily from the bike in the event of a crash. You will also be able to put a foot down as an outrigger if you are looking for extra balance.

5 Look well ahead so that you can see the best possible line. If you see an obstacle on the track ahead note it, in order to avoid it, but do not stare at it because you will hit it. Look where you want to go, not where you don't want to go.

6 Position your hands on the bars in as wide a grip as possible. This will give you more control if you need to get out of a rut or change your line. It will also give you a good chance of recovery should you hit a bump that knocks you off line.

Tackling obstacles

Off-road riding is not just a matter of going up and down hills and around corners. You will have to negotiate your way over and around plenty of obstacles on the way. As you ride more and more trails you will master new skills and will learn by experience which is the best way to tackle obstacles. Carry your bike if a section of the trail is unrideable.

Lifting the front wheel

1 Put the bike into a low gear when you are learning how to lift the front wheel. Slide your weight back slightly to the back of the saddle, bend low over the bike and lower your elbows. Position your stronger leg at the top of the pedal revolution.

2 Push down with your stronger leg and pull the handlebars up towards your chest at the same time. The front wheel will come well up off the ground. Lifting the wheel like this is the first step of many off-road maneuvers you will do.

CARRYING YOUR BIKE

At some time, you will come across terrain that is unrideable, or that you do not want to ride across, and you will have to carry your bike. The best way to carry your bike is with the frame across your right shoulder so that your body does not come into contact with the crankset. Put your right arm underneath and around the top tube. Hold the left handlebar grip with your right hand to keep the front wheel steady.

FALLING

Due to the unpredictable nature of off-road riding, it is inevitable that at some stage you will crash. Crashes are generally not as painful as they look, and you can usually avoid serious injury. Let go of the bike as soon as you know that you are going to crash. Aim for a soft place to land, avoid any trees, and try to go into a roll that takes you away from the bike.

Natural hazards

Part of the fun of mountain biking is riding over a wide range of natural obstacles and surfaces. There are different techniques for coping with these, which you should learn. If you intend to ride off-road regularly, and try out new areas, you are guaranteed to come across the full range. Do not be afraid to try something for the first time. Try to ride correctly and take it carefully.

BIG STUFF
When you come across a major obstacle, check it out before riding over it, and if in any doubt, carry your bike across. If you are confident that you can negotiate the obstacle, decide where to approach and where to land, and get up enough speed to carry you over safely. Do not stop halfway because this can be dangerous.

Jumping a log

1 Do not approach the log too fast. Reduce your speed so that you are in control. If you think the log is too big for you to cope with, stop now.

2 As you approach the log, compress your body weight down and jerk your handlebars rapidly up. Keep looking ahead. Your front wheel will lift.

3 Make sure that you lift the front wheel high enough to go over the log, otherwise you are likely to take the full impact of it and crash.

ROCKS

The best way to negotiate a rocky surface is to stand up out of the saddle and let the bike move underneath you as you ride across the rocks. If you restrict the bike at all, it will probably come to a standstill.

TREE ROOTS

Take great care going over tree roots because they can be very slippery when wet. Do not brake or accelerate hard over them. They are best negotiated in a similar way to rocks, letting the bike trail underneath you, with your arms and legs absorbing the bumps.

4 As the front wheel lands on the other side, you will feel the crankset hit the log. Shift your weight to the front of the bike to stop the crankset from bringing you to a halt.

5 The back wheel will begin to go over the log. Move your weight back to help put the wheel down on the ground. Keep your knees bent to absorb the landing.

6 When you are clear of the log, take up your normal position and resume pedalling. With practice, you will be able to do this maneuver without stopping.

Mud

You will definitely encounter mud while mountain biking. It is important when you do meet some, that you use the correct technique for riding through it. You can easily get stuck if it is very deep.

1 As you approach mud, shift your weight back to avoid going over the handlebars if the bike stops. Just before the mud, do a front wheel lift.

2 Once both your wheels are in the mud, keep pedalling to maintain momentum. If you do not you will come to a standstill and get stuck.

Water

You are quite likely at some stage to encounter a river or stream when riding off-road. Every stretch of water is different, so use the basic technique and adapt it according to the conditions that you find.

1 Before you ride into an unfamiliar river, reduce your speed. You do not know how deep it is or whether the riverbed is stones, mud or rock. Shift into a low gear then lift the front wheel into the water.

2 When you land, look for the best line across the river and start pedalling. If you are in a low enough gear you will have enough power to start moving quickly.

Sand

Sand can be very tricky to ride over, for two main reasons. Firstly, it has an amazing ability to sap your energy and power, and secondly, it is difficult to steer through because it causes the front wheel to change direction unexpectedly.

1 Enter a section of sand as fast as possible. It is amazing how quickly you lose speed in sand. Start in a high gear then change down when you hit the sand.

2 When the front wheel goes into sand it can pull the handlebars out of your control. To prevent this, keep a loose wide grip on the handlebars. This will allow them to move without throwing you off.

3 Try to stay on the surface of the mud and not sink into it. You can do this by using a very buoyant pedalling style, staying out of the saddle and lunging the bike forwards.

4 As you come to dry ground, heave the bike forwards. Pull it out of the mud by shifting your weight forwards which will help you to get the back wheel out.

3 Keep moving to avoid your back wheel digging a hole in the riverbed if it is soft. Lunge forwards with your bike, pedalling at the same time until you reach the bank.

4 As you hit the opposite bank, increase your pedalling speed to get out of the river. Your tires will be wet and may spin. To help avoid this, keep your weight low to put pressure on the tires.

3 As you slow down, change to a low standing position because the bike will move a lot underneath you. Pedal frantically in a low gear, and try to take a straight path through the sand.

4 It is vital to take care! Sand can throw your steering out very quickly. But at least you will have something soft to land on!

Steep stuff and edges

As you do more mountain biking, your skills will improve, and you will be able to take on the challenge of some advanced riding. Do not just head straight down every steep slope you come across. There is a trick to riding down steep stuff and some important rules to remember. If you do not apply these properly you could end up in a mangled heap at the bottom. Practise the technique on more gentle slopes then, as you perfect it, you can enjoy the thrill of going over an edge, confident in your ability to remain in control and pedal away at the bottom.

GOING DOWN
Looking over the edge of a steep drop-off can be quite daunting and may give you a rush of adrenalin. This is all part of the thrill of mountain biking.

Dropping off

1 The most important thing to remember when going over a drop-off is to sit well back over the back wheel. This will stop you from going over the handlebars and will improve your traction when braking.

2 Use your back brake to control your speed as you go over. Your center of gravity will be much higher than normal, and if you use your front brake it is very likely that you will be catapulted forwards over the handlebars.

1 Before going over the edge of a steep slope, be totally confident that you can negotiate the descent. If not, find a less difficult slope. Take a short run up to the slope at a controlled speed. This will give you time to get in to position.

Hopping up

1 If you have to get over a lip at the top of a slope, climb up to about 1 yard away from the edge.

2 Stop pedalling and position the pedals so that the cranks are horizontal. Pull the front wheel up quickly towards your chest, making sure that it clears the lip properly and lands on the ledge.

3 As your front wheel lands on the ledge, transfer your weight from the back of the bike to the front, and dab your front brake at the same time. This will instantly raise the rear wheel and bring it over the lip and on to the ledge.

4 Straighten your arms, push your weight back and release your front brake. This will push the rear wheel down on to the ground and back under your control. Take up your normal riding position and continue.

Descending steep slopes

2 Put your weight well over the back of the bike, have your pedals level and hold the handlebars with a wide grip. Look well ahead as you go over the edge of the descent, and do not brake suddenly. You are now committed to going down.

3 Your speed will increase rapidly, but do not brake suddenly because this is the thing most likely to make you crash. Your speed will help you if you go over any bumps during the descent, because your momentum will carry you over them.

4 It is common for a steep descent to be followed by a small rise. To be ready for this, bend down just as you reach the bottom of the slope. If you don't, the back wheel can be thrown up suddenly, which may cause you to crash.

In the air

Jumping with a bike is not only great fun, it is also a very useful technique to know. There will be times when you have to jump to get over an obstacle that you come across suddenly. There will also be times when you find yourself in the air unexpectedly, and it is important to know how to handle the bike in this situation.

Using the bunny hop to lift the bike over a branch.

Bunny hopping

1 As you are riding along, look ahead to where you are intending to bunny hop. Before you get there, bend down over the bike to keep your weight low, and level your cranks.

2 When you want to jump, spring your body up, pulling on the handlebars at the same time. As the front wheel comes off the ground, consciously lift your legs and feet to raise the rear wheel.

3 As you begin to come back down, relax your arms and legs to help absorb the shock of landing.

4 Try to land on both wheels at the same time, by keeping your weight over both wheels as you come down.

Dropping in

1 This is a useful technique for going over a steep edge smoothly and at speed. Keep your cranks level and lift the front wheel off the ground as you go over the edge.

2 As you are going through the air, look for where you are about to land and relax your arms and legs to help absorb the impact of landing.

3 Landing from a jump is hard on your bike. By remaining relaxed you will lighten the landing and reduce the chance of damaging your bike.

IN THE AIR

Remember that you are heavier than your bike and have more momentum. It is therefore important that you keep your weight low during a jump so that you and the bike do not go in different directions in the air. Never pull the brakes in the air because you will crash heavily on landing.

LANDING

There are two important rules to remember when landing from a jump. Always land on both wheels at the same time because a heavy front wheel landing can bend the forks or front wheel. Keep your body relaxed to absorb the landing and reduce the chance of damaging yourself or your bike.

BIG AIR

Once you have mastered the basics of jumping, you can have lots of fun and you can use it as a technique for clearing many obstacles on the trail. Always wear a helmet and gloves because crashes are more likely when you are jumping.

Tricks for the town

Riding your bike in the town can be more hazardous than off-road riding. Make sure that you know the rules of the road, and do not try to save time by taking

risks, such as running the lights, or riding the wrong way down a one-way street. Keep your wits about you and be ready to take emergency action should you need to.

Negotiating pot-holes

1 If you have a choice, do not ride through a pot-hole. It could result in your being catapulted over the handlebars, or your tire being punctured. Try to lift at least your front wheel over the hole by doing a front wheel lift. If the pot-hole is very deep you may prefer to do a bunny hop over it, but do this only if you are confident you can do it well.

2 When you come to the hole, lift your front wheel up and plant it back on the road the other side of the hole. When the wheel is down, put as much of your weight as possible on it, to reduce the impact on the rear wheel as it goes into the pot-hole. When both wheels have passed the hole, take up your normal position again.

Going up a curb

1 You should not ride on the sidewalk but there will be times when you have to go up the curb, for example to avoid having an accident or to get swiftly out of the way of traffic. You should therefore know how to do it quickly and safely.

2 Approach the curb from any angle but be careful if the pavement is wet because it can be very slippery. Bring your arms down and do a front wheel lift (see page 98), making sure that the wheel clears the curb.

3 Put the front wheel down firmly on the sidewalk. Push your weight back and dab the front brake to lift the rear wheel off the ground. Do not let the wheel hit the curb under your full weight because you could damage your wheel.

4 With your front wheel on the sidewalk, and your rear wheel in the air, push the bike forwards underneath you and let the rear wheel land on the sidewalk. Relax your arms and legs to give yourself a smooth landing.

CHAPTER 6

Races and events

There is nothing quite like the thrill of competing whether in a race or to get into the record books. There are thousands of mountain bike events every year for professional and amateur riders. Whatever their age and ability, everyone will find a suitable competition to enter if they want to. One of the most fascinating aspects of competition is the part that it plays in the development of the sport, as manufacturers and riders strive to improve their designs and techniques.

Cross-country

Anyone can enter a cross-country race because the races cater to a wide range of abilities. Most races take place on a circuit between 3 and 8 miles long with racers in different categories having to complete a different number of laps. Races can be anything from 10 to 140 miles long. Cross-country racing combines all the elements of mountain biking – steep descents, high-speed cornering and gruelling climbs – on a mixture of different tracks and surfaces.

THE START
On the start line, everyone tries to get a good position with space around them, so that they can start without hindrance. It is quite normal for there to be a lot of elbowing and shouting when the gun goes off as the riders try to get to the front. Mountain bike races are notorious for getting off to a fast start and only more experienced racers will know how to emerge from this unscathed.

Tires must be suitable for the conditions. Most racers do not decide which type to use until they get to the race course.

UP AND DOWNHILL
Cross-country races always incorporate a series of demanding climbs and downhills to test the ability of the racers. The best riders pace themselves so that they do not run out of steam over the last few laps.

WINNING
It is a fantastic feeling when you win a race. Being physically drained but ecstatic is an intoxicating mix. Usually, it is the more experienced racers who win, and not just the fittest. They ride smoothly, anticipate gear changes and avoid crashes.

ORIENTEERING

If you do not want to thrash it out with hundreds of riders together, you may prefer an orienteering event. These test your map reading and stamina but require less physical fitness. Riders set off in pairs at two-minute intervals and try to find different check points where they collect points. The more difficult the check point is to find, the more points it is worth. The goal is to accumulate as many points as possible. Speed is not everything. By going too quickly a rider may miss a vital turn.

READY TO RACE

A bike must be set up carefully before a race so that it is in perfect working order.

A narrow saddle allows the rider to slip off the back easily when approaching a steep drop-off.

Handlebars have to have plugs at either end to prevent them from injuring someone in a crash.

Racing yourself

If you are thinking about taking up racing, do it. It is great fun, and there are plenty of events that you can enter which are friendly and not at all intimidating. To start with, cross-country racing is the best type for you to do. There are categories for the complete novice and the professional, and for everybody in between. Once you have tried it you may well get hooked.

NOTHING SPECIAL

To start racing you don't need to have the most sophisticated bike. You will find that people race on bikes of all ages and qualities. The only piece of equipment that you will definitely need is a helmet that meets the approved safety standard. If you do not wear one you may not be covered by the promoters' insurance in the event of an accident, and you may not be allowed to race without one.

Pockets on the back of a jersey are useful for carrying your tool kit and race food.

Padded Lycra cycling shorts

Check that all bolts and clamps are tightened up securely.

RACING FOR FUN

Many large events are held each year which are aimed at 'fun' riders including children. There is usually a friendly and welcoming atmosphere and the whole family can take part. Before you set off for an event make sure that you know exactly where it is and what time your race is. Events are often held in remote areas and can be difficult to find.

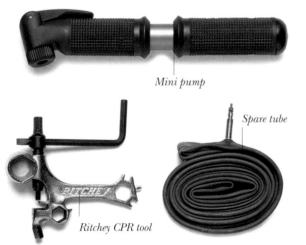

Mini pump

Spare tube

Ritchey CPR tool

RACING TOOL KIT

Take only essential tools with you on the race. The most likely damage you will have is a puncture, so take a spare inner tube with a Presta valve, a spare tire, two tire levers and a pump. Other than these, take only a Ritchey CPR tool, which can be useful, and a section of spare chain links in case you damage your chain.

RACING TIPS

Take plenty of water with you on the race. It is also a good idea to drink about seven cups of water a day for a week before the race, to make sure that you are fully hydrated. To help your race to go smoothly, and to give you a chance to do well, prepare properly so that there are no last-minute panics. Check that your bike is mechanically sound at least two days before the race. Ride the course in advance to get a feel for it, and arrive at the starting line in plenty of time.

RACING CHECKLIST

Bike	In full working order
Helmet	The correct standard
Shoes	Suitable for the event and comfortable
Papers	Number, licence, and any instructions
Tool kit	Essential items for minor repairs
Food and drink	Enough water and energy food for the whole race
Clothing	Comfortable clothing including a waterproof jacket and a change of clothing for after the race
Cleaning materials	Bucket and brush for taking mud off the bike after the race

ENTERING RACES

Most races are advertised in mountain bike magazines. They can be extremely popular so try to enter at least three weeks in advance to guarantee getting a place. For many races you will need a license. If you are just doing one race you can get a day license, but if you want to take part in several races, it is cheaper to get a one-year license by joining NORBA (National Off-Road Bicycle Association). Pick up an application at your bike shop, or write: USA Cycling, One Olympic Plaza, Colorado Springs, CO 80909.

Choose your tires to suit the conditions on the race course.

Downhill

Downhill racing is becoming increasingly popular among spectators as well as competitors. The combination of speed, jumps and the occasional spectacular crash, make it a great spectator sport. With speeds of up to 60 mph on certain courses, it is also generating huge media interest, and is currently attracting lots of sponsorship. The downhill racers have a unique, outlandish style. Many people think that they are crazy, but they are highly skilled and very aware of the dangers involved.

MADE FOR THE JOB

As downhill racing becomes more and more popular, manufacturers are producing bikes that are purely for downhill racing, always trying to improve the speed and safety of the rider. The bikes now offer anything from 2 to 6 inches of suspension travel, use front and rear disc brakes, and have moto-cross-style handlebars.

CRASHING OUT

There are very few serious accidents during races, but the chance of having a high-speed crash is a risk that downhill racers take. All serious racers will have crashed in at least one of their races, and most will have had a serious injury. This does not seem to put people off, because the thrill of racing outweighs the fear of getting hurt, and medical help is always at hand if a crash does occur.

▼TECHNICAL TESTS

As well as going downhill, the course for a race normally incorporates a series of technical corners and spectacular jumps to test the skill of the riders and not just their speed. Huge crowds gather near these parts of the course to try to catch a glimpse of their downhill heroes flying through the air.

▲DOWNHILL PROTECTION

Certain pieces of equipment are essential for downhill racing as protection. As well as a helmet to protect the head, special gloves with padding on both sides are worn to protect the hands in the event of a crash. Goggles are vital to keep wind and dust out of the eyes. Other pieces of equipment that an increasing number of serious downhill racers wear are full-faced helmets, elbow and knee pads and other padding.

Dual slalom and observed

These mountain bike events are highly entertaining. The riders have to tackle obstacles or jumps, and dual slalom riders also have to ride at speed. Dual slaloms are normally held at a major event after the 'serious' races have taken place. The races are uncategorized so fun riders and juniors get the chance to thrash it out against professionals. Trials are normally categorized from novice to pro-expert. Sadly, not enough regular events are held to help trials to gain the status of other mountain bike events, although there are many dedicated and sponsored riders.

Dual slalom

ELIMINATION

A dual slalom event is run on an elimination system. There can be up to 60 competitors in the original field, which gets whittled down to the final two. At each stage, the competitors race twice, once down each set of poles. The winner is the one who is best over the two runs.

A TIGHT LINE

The racers take as tight a line as possible around the slalom poles, often getting so close that they have to hit the pole away with their arm. Most slalom racers wear some form of arm padding to protect their arms if they hit a pole hard.

HEAD TO HEAD

In dual slalom, two competitors race against each other down a short course which bends and twists around a series of poles. Most races start through timing gates. Sometimes there is a large metal ramp which drops down, propelling the riders forwards.

DOWN BUT NOT OUT

Due to the speed and technicality of the courses there are always some crashes. Racers who crash still have a chance of winning their race, if they can get up quickly, because there is a high chance that their opponent will crash too.

JUMPS TOO

The courses normally include some spectacular jumps to make the races more difficult. These are fun for the spectators to watch, as riders fling themselves through the air, trying to lose as little time as possible.

rials

Observed trials

BALANCE NOT SPEED
In observed trials, competitors have to ride over or around a series of obstacles without putting a foot down. This is the one mountain bike event where speed is not important.

TECHNICAL SKILL
Negotiating the obstacles requires skill and concentration. An accomplished trials rider will be able to ride over almost anything from a 15-foot vertical drop-off to a car.

TRUE MOUNTAIN BIKING
Many trials riding techniques will come in useful during a normal off-road ride when you may suddenly encounter an obstacle.

DEMONSTRATION
Observed trials riders are often employed to show off their skill at other events. The promise of some spectacular riding pulls in the crowds.

SCORING
When a competitor puts a foot down it is called a dab. Every dab scores a point. The competitor with the lowest score wins.

The professionals

To be a fully sponsored professional is the goal of many racers. Besides the excitement of it, the main benefit is the substantial financial and technical support that is available throughout the season. The level of back-up can make the difference between winning and losing. The biggest, most successful teams have large budgets helped by co-sponsors, and the racers have the help of mechanics, masseurs and managers.

Lightweight OCLV carbon fiber frame weighs 2.88 pounds.

RACERS

To an outsider, the life of a professional racer looks like a glamorous one, with hours spent riding the latest machine and being paid a six-figure salary to do so. The reality is very different. When they are not out of action through injury, most racers spend months training hard and hours cramped up in the back of a truck driving to races, only to be beaten by a fraction of a second.

MECHANIC

Every good team is supported by a mechanic. He or she is responsible for making sure that the racers' bikes are set up perfectly and are mechanically sound. The worst thing that can happen to a mechanic is when the team leader has DNF (did not finish) on the result sheet due to a mechanical failure. There are many stories of mechanics being sacked by racers in rage, after the bikes they had worked on failed during an important race.

TREK TEAM BIKE

This Trek Pro Issue is the same bike that was ridden by the Trek team throughout the Grundig, the NORBA National Championship Series and World Cup racing series.

Front suspension fork supplied by Rock Shox.

SPONSORSHIP

Due to the high-speed action and thrills and spills of mountain biking, television coverage of the sport is increasing and it is regarded by manufacturers as a good opportunity to advertise. There has recently been an explosion in lucrative sponsorship deals, and riders now have logos on their bike and their clothes.

TRANSPORT

A mountain bike team can consist of anything up to eight riders, 30 bikes, two mechanics, a masseur, a cook and a team manager. All these have to be transported from one event to the next, and due to the nature of mountain biking, events are nearly always a long drive away. The current trend is to customize a box van, turning it into a vehicle that will carry the whole team and everything they might need. There is huge competition between teams to turn up in the biggest and baddest vehicle.

The big races

As in most sports, there are some mountain bike events that are considered to be more important than others. These major races are the ones that everyone wants to win. They attract huge media and public attention every year, and a racer's performance can be the deciding factor behind a large sponsorship deal being confirmed or taken away. Careers are made here – and shattered.

CHAMPION RACER
The most successful cross-country world champion to date is Henrik Djernis. He has the ability to time his training so that he is at the peak of his fitness for the World Championships, and has won three in a row. Many people said that his first two wins were lucky and not due to skill. He silenced his critics in 1994 when he won his third championship in Vail, Colorado, on a tough course at high altitude.

DOWNHILL
This is the event of the moment. It is drawing huge crowds and is being shown on many television networks as an extreme sport. There is concern that some of the downhill courses are too dangerous and are pushing the riders too near the limit of their ability. Most racers now wear body padding and full-faced helmets as protection, in an attempt to prevent serious injury in a crash.

▶ WORLD CUP SERIES

The World Cup is a competition between riders from Europe and the USA. It takes place over a period of about eight months in a variety of countries. Racers gain points according to their position in each race, and the rider with the highest total at the end of the season becomes the World Cup champion. Races include downhills and cross-country, and the most notorious race is the downhill held at Cap d'Ail in the south of France. The course goes down near-vertical donkey tracks, over huge boulders and around hairpin bends. It has one of the highest percentages of DNFs (did not finish) of the World Cup and it is quite common for at least one rider to need air-lifting from the scene.

▲ WORLD CHAMPIONSHIPS

This is the event that every mountain bike racer wants to win. It takes place over 10 days in a different country every year. The course is thoroughly checked by cycling's international governing body, the *Union Cyclist Internationale* (UCI) to make sure that it has all the necessary elements to make a demanding world class course. It has to include long sections of technical singletrack, a climb at altitude, technical fast downhills and many different surfaces.

Bike extremists

When mountain biking first started in Southern California, it was considered to be a wild and wacky thing to do. Today it is accepted as one of the cycling sports, but there is still an extreme element. People attempt near-impossible feats on mountain bikes, riding at breath-taking speeds, performing incredible stunts, and pushing themselves and their bikes to the limits of endurance.

IDITA BIKE

This event is held in Alaska every year. It is a two-day race through snow and ice in which competitors have to carry all their own equipment including camping gear. It is one of the toughest races in the world, and it is an achievement just to finish. To cope with the conditions, the bikes have two sets of rims welded on to each other so that they can take extra-wide tires to help the bike stay on top of the snow. They have extra tire clearance to accommodate these tires and many bikes have hub brakes.

HANS REY

Some trials riders go to extremes, and Hans Rey is one of the best trials riders in the world. He leaps and jumps over and across obstacles and seems to defy gravity. He will try anything, from riding off a 20-foot vertical drop to clearing the gap between two huge boulders.

DOWNHILL SPEED RECORD

An increasingly popular challenge for the speed merchants of the mountain biking world is the downhill speed record, currently standing at more than 111 mph set by Christian Taillefer. Record attempts are usually made on ski runs with hard-packed snow. The bikes have metal-spiked tires, aerodynamic streamlining, disc brakes and front and rear suspension. The riders wear aerodynamic suits and sleek full-faced helmets. Shown here is Giovanna Bonazzi, who set the women's record of 89 mph at the same event.

EXTREME CONDITIONS

Mountain biking across Africa is hard enough on an ordinary mountain bike, but these fanatics decided to do it on a unique three-seater bike! Their journey from Botswana to Egypt covered 7,000 miles and raised money for African and children's charities. This is just one of many incredible expeditions embarked upon by those who wish to push mountain biking to its limits. No terrain provides a barrier to the extreme mountain biker.

CHAPTER 7

Get up and go

Mountain biking is not just an exciting sport, it is also one of the best ways to spend your holiday. Cycling is a relatively cheap way to travel, and because mountain bikes are designed to go off-road, you can get to many places that other travellers will never see. Whether you want to see a country, or just some new mountain trails; whether you plan a long expedition or a short stay, let your mountain bike take you. You will see some of the most beautiful and remote areas of the world, and probably few other tourists.

Great Britain

Even though Great Britain is relatively small it contains some of the most beautiful and varied terrain. There are some unique areas of countryside which are perfect for off-road riding, such as the Scottish Highlands, the South Downs and Snowdonia. These places are popular with hikers too, because of the spectacular scenery. It is important that you ride with consideration for them and take care of the fragile environment.

DARTMOOR

Dartmoor is an area of approximately 200 square miles of open moorland in southwest England. Most of the area is about 700 feet high with the highest point about 2,000 feet. It is a unique area covered in heather and broom with amazing granite rock formations and many bogs. It is fairly inhospitable on a bad day but at the same time incredibly striking, with many beautiful isolated spots. It is very exposed, so sudden weather changes are common and it can be dangerous if you get lost.

SOUTH DOWNS

The South Downs are a continuous ridge of hills which runs along the south coast of England. They are approximately 100 miles long and offer many different rides. There are amazing views on both sides and it is possible on a good day to see the whole length of the Downs ahead of you. If you are planning to ride a long section, try to ride with the wind behind you because it can be quite hard to ride against it. The Downs are popular with walkers, especially on weekends, so be careful.

◄ SCOTTISH HIGHLANDS

One of the best things about Scotland is that it has a huge range of areas in which you can ride off-road. Because much of the land is termed 'common land' you can legally ride almost anywhere, and it is quite likely that you will not meet anyone else all day. Fort William is a good place to base yourself. It is at the base of Ben Nevis from where you can get spectacular views. When riding in this area, remember that much of it is exposed and there is little habitation.

SCOTTISH BORDERS

The Scottish Borders offer some dramatic scenery and a wide range of terrain. There are many large areas of forest, such as Kielder Forest, where the Forestry Commission actively encourages the use of mountain bikes.

WALES

Wales offers a huge variety of terrain for mountain biking, with lots of hills from Snowdonia to the Brecon Beacons. There are also many forestry commission areas where mountain biking is encouraged. Wales is not very accessible by motorway. This means that much of it is still unspoiled but it can take hours to get there. Wales is renowned for being wet, so always take waterproof clothing.

◄ LAKE DISTRICT

The Lake District is unique in many ways due to its glaciated mountain formations. It is strikingly beautiful and offers some of the most demanding riding in Great Britain. It attracts millions of people and this puts huge pressure on the environment. Be very careful where and how you ride because trail erosion is a major problem. Some specially created mountain bike trails are beginning to be opened.

► PEAK DISTRICT AND YORKSHIRE DALES

The Peak District and Yorkshire Dales offer some picturesque and technically demanding terrain. The Peak District has suffered for its popularity and some routes are badly eroded so you may find that mountain bikes are not allowed in certain places. The Yorkshire Dales are far more open with fewer restrictions on where you can ride. Many large, forested areas, such as Dolby Forest, actively encourage recreational use.

The mountains of Europe

The spectacular scenery of the Alps, Pyrenees, and Dolomites has thrilled skiers for years. Now the mountains are becoming popular destinations for mountain bikers. Many ski resorts become mountain bike resorts in the summer and have marked routes. Many of these are graded, rather like ski runs, catering for people of varying abilities. You can usually find a local guide who will take you on the best routes. Alternatively, some small companies offer guided mountain bike holidays.

◀ Mt. Blanc and the area around Chamonix is one of the best places in the Alps for mountain biking. Chamonix offers great night life if you've any strength left after your ride.

▼ PYRENEES

The Pyrenees cover a smaller area than the Alps but still offer some amazing riding. The main characteristics of this area are steep valleys and rock strewn hillsides, and long routes which take you just down- or uphill for up to 12 miles. There are fewer lifts than in the Alps because there are fewer ski resorts.

▲ FRENCH AND SWISS ALPS

The French and Swiss Alps are popular with mountain bikers because they contain some of the most spectacular routes in Europe. You can follow marked routes that climb high up into the mountains and find some steep and technically demanding descents. Most of the ski resorts will allow you to take your bike on the back of the chair lifts and in cable cars. Therefore, if you want to, you can ride just downhill.

AUSTRIAN ALPS AND ITALIAN DOLOMITES

These two areas have a completely different look and feel from the French and Swiss Alps. The Dolomites are made up of huge limestone outcrops and are spectacular. Access for mountain bikes in both these areas is not widespread, or clearly marked. Get a local guidebook and check before you go so that you do not arrive somewhere only to discover you are not allowed to ride your bike there.

The Mediterranean

In most Mediterranean countries there is some excellent off-road riding in spectacular scenery. Many good mountain biking locations are within easy reach of an airport and there are few problems with access. In many places you will be able to find a guide to show you the best routes, or you can go on an organized trip that provides support on the trail. It can get extremely hot so you may not be able to ride during the hottest part of the day, but there are plenty of other sports and sights to keep you busy.

▲ SPAIN AND CANARY ISLANDS

Spain is such a large country that it has many different types of terrain. One of the most beautiful areas to ride in is the Andalucian mountains in the Sierra Nevada. Spain has a rich history, and visiting the fascinating sights makes a break if the temperature gets too high for riding. The Canary Islands are volcanic islands off the coast of Spain. They are covered in a network of trails offering a good range of riding, but you must pick the right time to go because it can get extremely hot.

▶ MOROCCO

The best riding in this huge country is in the Anti Atlas and the High Atlas mountains where there are peaks over 13,000 feet high. It can get extremely hot here and you will often be riding far away from civilization. The best way to go to Morocco is through a bike tour operator that provides food and water and 4-wheel drive support.

ITALY AND SARDINIA

Riding in Italy is great because on the whole the Italians love cyclists. You will find many places to eat and drink, and you will be made to feel very welcome. Riding is fun around Lake Garda because there are many good routes around the lakes, and other sports to do, such as sailing and windsurfing. There is always a nice cool breeze to stop you from getting too hot. Sardinia is covered in a network of old donkey trails on which you can ride. These are technically quite demanding but also great fun.

TURKEY

One of the best regions to ride in Turkey is Cappadocia. A combination of earthquakes, volcanic eruptions and weathering has created an amazing landscape. There are many networks of paths and trails and fascinating historical sites to visit. It is best to travel with a guide and some support. Roads in Turkey can be dangerous for cycling, so try to keep off-road as much as possible.

CRETE

This Greek island is very similar in temperature and terrain to Sardinia. It is best to ride in the morning, when the temperature is lower, and relax in the afternoon. The island has a wealth of history which will keep you entertained if it gets too hot.

COTE D'AZUR

If you want to mix mountain biking with luxury and glamour, this may be the place to go. Behind the coastal strip there is scope for extensive off-road riding. You can sample the notorious World Cup downhill course at Cap d'Ail if you dare. Be sure you have plenty of money because this area is extremely expensive.

North America

The varied terrain here has made the mountain bike what it is today. There are deserts, forests, grasslands and incredible mountains, and it is quite possible, if you are in the right place, to ride through most of these environments on one day's ride. The disadvantage of riding in the United States is that mountain bikers have restricted access to the off-road trails, and many areas are closed to them altogether. Instead, there are specific parks which cater to mountain bike use.

▲ ROCKY MOUNTAINS

The Rocky Mountains stretch from Colorado to Canada. Some of the best riding in the Rockies is in the southwest, around the town of Durango, Colorado. This has become one of the 'Meccas' of mountain biking. It is surrounded by huge networks of trails and some amazing scenery. Durango is located where the Rockies meet the New Mexico desert, which means that you can be riding through beautiful aspen trees one day and be surrounded by cacti the next.

◀ MOAB, UTAH

Moab is one of the most spectacular areas for riding in the world. It is a huge orange rock, which weathering has turned into one of the mountain biking wonders of the world. Its smooth undulating surface gives you amazing grip, making it possible to climb or traverse at any angle, and it is covered with natural jumps, dips and exciting descents.

NORTHERN CALIFORNIA

This is where mountain biking originated and you can see why the sport developed so quicky. Unfortunately, many of the great trails that were used by the pioneers are no longer open to mountain bikers, and there is a speed restriction of 15 mph on most trails that are open.

BIG BEAR AND MAMMOTH, CALIFORNIA

These are two ski resorts which cater to mountain bikers in the summer. They are privately owned and no other trail users can get in. You can buy a mountain bike pass which will give you unlimited riding and use of ski lifts, and the different trails are graded in technical abililty just like ski runs. Both these locations have major races during the season. Mammoth is host to one of the most popular downhill races, called the Mammoth Kamikaze.

BAJA CALIFORNIA, MEXICO

This is the finger of land that stretches south of California. It is part of Mexico and is becoming a popular destination for American mountain bikers. Baja California offers similar terrain to California but does not have the same restrictions on where and how fast you can ride.

SKI LIFTS

Many American ski resorts now cater to mountain bikes during their off season. It is a great attraction to be able to carry your bike up on the back of a chair lift rather than have to endure the long slog of climbing, even though the latter would make you fitter.

Africa and Asia

Several tour operators organize mountain biking trips to Africa and Asia. These are ideal if you would prefer to ride with support rather than explore on your own. Make sure that you have the right inoculations before you go, and carry a well-equipped medical kit containing relevant items for the area where you are going. As long as you are sensible, you will enjoy some incredible rides.

▶ NEPAL

Nepal has been welcoming cyclists for about 10 years and mountain biking in the Himalayas has become a popular alternative to walking. Over the centuries, trails have been built in the upper valleys and mountains for humans and yaks, with many steps cut into the stone. It is possible to ride a mountain bike here but be prepared to carry it in places. The scenery is magnificent, the air sweet and the people extremely friendly. If you want to camp and do not want to take your equipment with you, you can buy it all, including a bike, in the capital, Kathmandu. In the southern plain of Nepal, an area of jungle bordering the Chitwan National Park also provides some exciting mountain bike trails.

AFRICA

Africa is a diverse continent and some countries within it are popular for mountain bike riding. The most tourist-friendly are Kenya, Tanzania and South Africa. Before travelling, make sure that the country is reasonably stable and that you have the correct visas. It is a good idea when you get there to inform your embassy where you are going and when you expect to return.

INDIA

The Himalayan foothills are in northern India and these are ideal for mountain biking. The state of Himachal Pradesh contains pine forests, alpine meadows and beautiful valleys such as the Manali valley. Through a pass from Manali, into Jammu and Kashmir, is the Ladakh mountain range at just over 12,000 feet – one of the most beautiful places on earth. There are wonderful rides here, as you enter a world of monasteries, prayer flags and yaks. Be careful to drink lots because the air is extremely dry and it is easy to get dehydrated. In the south of India, the Nilgiri Hills, on the border between the states of Karnataka and Tamil Nadu, are also ideal for mountain biking.

Australia and New Zealand

From tropical rain forests to snowy peaks, from massive deserts to rolling fields, these countries together offer the mountain biker an enormous range of scenery and terrain. Outdoor pursuits are a popular pastime and you should feel welcome wherever you go. Choose the time of year for a trip carefully, because if you go at the wrong time it can be too hot or too wet. And don't forget your helmet because the wearing of one is a legal requirement.

AUSTRALIA

Mountain biking is becoming increasingly popular in Australia, particularly in New South Wales, Queensland and Victoria, and there is a wide variety of riding terrain. As well as hot desert and bush, Australia also has high snow-capped mountains. Some guidebooks are available, and you should ask in bike shops for advice on the good routes. You will not be allowed on a train with your bike unbagged, but you can usually buy a bike box at the station.

SNOWY MOUNTAINS

If you prefer cool weather, you should head for the Snowy Mountains, which are about seven hours' drive west of Sydney. These are used by skiers in the winter and offer good mountain biking terrain in the summer with extensive trails and ski lifts.

NEW ZEALAND

Everything a mountain biker could desire can be found in New Zealand. It is perfect for mountain biking. Most of the country is still unspoiled and there are few people and few cars. There are lush green valleys, steep technical climbs, endless forest trails through national parks, and very few restrictions on where you can ride. Then, if you get bored on your bike you can go river-rafting, kayaking and bungee-jumping. You should take a full selection of wet weather clothing because it can be wet. There are lots of streams and rivers to cross and you may often get caught in a sudden downpour.

SOUTH ISLAND

New Zealand comprises two main islands. Most of the best riding is in South Island, which contains the Southern Alps. Mount Cook is over 12,000 feet high. Queenstown is a good base. It is situated by Lake Wakatipu and is ringed by snow-capped mountains. There is less risk of getting wet farther north. The Abel Tasman National Park in the northwest of South Island contains the Tasman mountains where there are good trails for mountain biking.

◄ Mountain biking at the Olgas, in the Australian outback. By no means is all Australian mountain biking so remote.

A big expedition

When you feel like getting away from it all, take your mountain bike on an expedition. The prospect of an adventure like this may be a bit daunting but, once you set off, you will enjoy it and after a few days in the saddle you will settle into a comfortable routine. There will be days which are tough and which you may not enjoy, but most of the time it will be exhilarating and the feeling of achievement you get will make it all worthwhile.

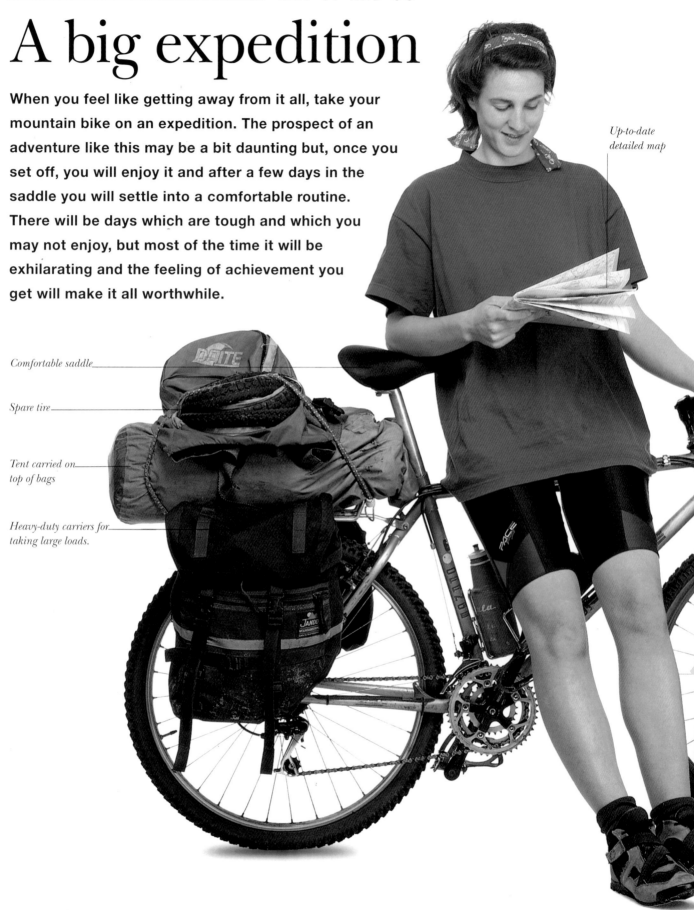

Up-to-date detailed map

Comfortable saddle

Spare tire

Tent carried on top of bags

Heavy-duty carriers for taking large loads.

KEEPING IN TOUCH

It is highly unlikely that you will have any major problems, but just in case, keep in regular contact with your family or friends. Let them know where you are heading, when you expect to be there and when you will try to contact them again. Let your embassy know your whereabouts too. Take the fax number of a bike shop that agrees to send any parts you ask for to advance destinations. Always keep your money, passport and important papers on your body to help prevent them from getting stolen.

Reliable thumbshifters

Large panniers for carrying clothing, food, water, tools and spare parts.

PLANNING

Once you have decided on your destination and the duration of your trip, make a rough plan of your route taking into account how far you think you can ride in a day. Allow yourself some days for staying put and exploring one area. Do some research and figure out how much money you will probably spend and add a third again to cover emergencies or a change of plan. Organize a system of transferring funds from home so that you do not have to carry large amounts of cash.

EQUIPMENT

If possible, take a straightforward bike with a steel frame because there is less to go wrong and a steel frame is easier to repair than an aluminum one. Get hand-built wheels with heavy spokes and take a spare tire and lots of spare spokes with you. Ask a bike shop what tools you should take for fixing your bike. Take comfortable clothing and a change of clothing for when you are not cycling. If you are camping, take a lightweight tent, sleeping bag and cooking equipment. When on the road, always carry extra food and an ample supply of water because you may not know where the next shop will be.

A year in South America

In August 1993, Emily Clowes set off with her mountain bike to cycle in South America. She flew to Lima in Peru and spent the next year travelling. She went almost from top to bottom of the continent, reaching Tierra del Fuego, the southern tip, in February 1994. She eventually returned home from Bogota in Colombia in August 1994. The trip was a fantastic experience. Emily met lots of people, both locals and fellow cyclists, and was able to see some of the most beautiful scenery in the world.

THE JOURNEY

Emily's trip through South America took her through a variety of terrains, climates and altitudes. She rode through mountains and deserts, across high plains and beside the sea. The most she covered in one day was a staggering 100 miles. The Atacama desert, the driest desert in the world, was difficult to cope with, as were the strong winds. Emily found it was best to start early in the morning, before the wind gathered strength.

THE BIKE

Fully laden, Emily's bike weighed 77-88 pounds depending on how much food and water she was carrying. The bike was an Orange Clockwork Mountain bike. All the parts were standard except for a more comfortable women's saddle and thumbshifters instead of Rapidfire. The only spare parts she carried were inner tubes and one tire. When she needed anything else she faxed a list to a shop at home with which she had made arrangements before she left. They sent the parts to an address she gave them where she knew she would be when they arrived.

Excerpts from Emily's diary

23 AUGUST 1993: COLEA CANYON, PERU

I am sitting on the edge of the Colea Canyon. It's 3:07 p.m. and the sun is still very hot even though in three hours it will be dark. If I had slipped getting here I could have fallen more than 10,000 feet into the Colea river, but I had to come to this spot. The canyon looks so beautiful. One day I will return with a tent and spend days here.

13 JANUARY 1994: SOUTHERN CHILE

We sat on the shores of Lake Buenos Aires watching an armadillo, then decided that we should keep going. I can't really complain about the wind today because for the most part it was behind us. Just an indication of how strong it was, it pushed me uphill without me having to pedal. It was rather like when you are surfing and catch a wave – suddenly, whoosh and you're off.

15 FEBRUARY 1994: TIERRA DEL FUEGO

It was cold, gray and windy as we cycled to the ferry which was to take us to 'Fire Land.' The crossing took just over two hours, then we set foot on Tierra del Fuego. After 32 miles we headed for the sea to celebrate. It was wonderful riding by the sea with the wind behind us. We sat in the sun and swigged champagne out of the bottle.

9 AUGUST 1994: CORDILLERA CENTRAL, COLOMBIA

I've cycled 89 miles and I'm shattered. My legs are shaking and three fingers on my left hand are numb. But I'm also content and in awe of the beautiful landscape. I was happy climbing and got rather bored going downhill afterwards except for the splendid views. The huge mountains plunged down to gorges that were so deep that I was unable to see the bottom. The land was dry and sun-scorched, and so was I.

Bogota

Lima

South	....
North	....

Solid rule is distance cycled
Dotted rule is public transportation

500 miles

THE PEOPLE

The local people were friendly and helpful. Some invited Emily to stay in their house because they were concerned for her safety if she camped outside. Cars and trucks would often stop because people were surprised to see a cyclist in the middle of nowhere and wanted to check that everything was OK. On one occasion the terrain was so severe and steep that it was impossible to ride across it. Luckily some passing locals gave Emily a lift in their truck.

CHAPTER 8

Basic bike maintenance

Mountain biking is very demanding on the mechanical parts of your bike, in comparison to road riding. The combination of mud, grit and water is a recipe for wear and tear. The bike also takes a huge pounding from the trail, resulting in damage such as wheels being knocked out of true and handlebars getting bent. You should be aware of which areas on your bike are vulnerable and be able to diagnose a problem when something goes wrong. Then you will be able to get any damage repaired promptly before it becomes a serious problem.

General checks

You may not be interested in working on your own bike but it is a good idea to be able to identify a mechanical problem if one develops. If you have to take your bike to a shop to get it repaired, you will get better service if you know yourself what needs doing. You will save the shop time, and will be able to check that the job has been done properly.

SEAT POST
Always make sure that your seat post is well greased where it goes into the frame. If it is not greased regularly, you may well find that it gets stuck in the frame and will be difficult and expensive to remove.

BRAKE BLOCKS
Check the toeing-in of your brake blocks. When toed in correctly, the brakes should work smoothly and almost silently.

TIRES
Check the tire pressure. The correct pressure is given on the sidewall of the tire. If the tires are too soft, they will feel sluggish. If they are too hard, the bike will vibrate.

SPROCKETS AND CHAIN
Keep the sprockets and chain sparkling clean. Clean them after every major ride and then relube them. Use a lube that is best suited to your riding conditions.

CHAINRINGS
Check that the chainring bolts are not loose or missing. If you lose one, replace it immediately because the chainring can bend at the point where the bolt is missing.

BOLTS
If you remove a bolt that has had Loctite applied, make sure you use Loctite again when you reassemble it. You can normally see when bolts have had this on because it leaves a blue residue on the bolt.

AFTER A CRASH

Spin both the wheels to check for trueness and check that your handlebar stem is straight. Lift the back wheel off the ground and move the pedals around to check that the chain is on and the gears are running smoothly.

CABLES

Keep all cables clean and lubricate them regularly. They are the vital link between the control levers and the brakes and gears. A badly neglected cable will seriously affect the shifting or braking performance.

Checking the frame

FORKS

Check to see if the forks are bent, especially if you have had a crash. The best way to check is from above. The top 6 inches of conventional forks should run parallel with the head tube. If the forks are bent the bike will feel odd to ride. You may clip the front wheel with your foot, and the handlebars will alternate between being stiff and loose.

TUBES

Inspect the place where the down tube, top tube and head tube meet. Look for cracking in the paint on the top of the top and down tubes, then run your finger underneath the tubes to feel for any ripples in the tube. If there are some, you will have no choice but to replace the frame.

DROPOUT

Check the rear dropout to see if it is bent or cracked. Most dropouts on steel frames can be restraightened. An aluminum frame should have a replaceable rear dropout. If the dropout is cracked where it joins the frame, ask a shop to inspect it for a possible manufacturing defect.

WHEELS

Make sure that the spokes are adjusted to the correct tension. Unequal tension is especially common with new wheels that have been ridden hard for several weeks.

BEARINGS

Check that the bearings in your hubs, bottom bracket, headset and pedals are tight. If something is loose in a bearing you will notice a vibration coming from the affected area.

Brakes

It is most important that your brakes are in good working order. If one fails suddenly, due to a cable breaking, for example, it could be extremely dangerous. Mountain biking is very demanding on the brakes. They are in constant use in extreme conditions. Grit gets stuck to the pads, and water and dirt get into the cables. Check all parts regularly and replace them when necessary for your own safety.

BRAKE WEAR

Adjust the position of the brake blocks as the pads wear. The pads should sit firmly on the rim of the wheels but, because a cantilever brake moves through an arc, the pads tend to slip off the rim and into the spokes as they wear down. Cantilever brakes are individually sprung, and it is important that the springs are on equal settings. If they are uneven, the brakes will have a tendency to pull to one side. Most brakes have an adjustment screw for fine-tuning the spring power.

CABLES

Check the brake cables regularly for signs of fraying. They normally fray at points of high friction and where the cable is bolted. Lubricate the cable to reduce the chances of fraying, and do not overtighten the anchor bolt. Over-tightening splays the cable, causing it to fray, and possibly break.

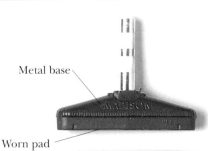

Metal base

Worn pad

BRAKE PADS

Keep an eye on the state of wear of the brake pads. If they wear down to the metal base, they will damage your rims. Release the link wire and inspect the surface of each pad. Remove the lip, which normally develops with wear on brake pads used with cantilevers. The lip will prevent the cantilever from releasing properly, causing the brake pad to drag on the rim.

LINK WIRE BRAKE

The link wire pulls the cantilever calipers together. Check that they are not kinked because, if they are, they will not pull properly. They should also be tight but not be too tight through the anchor bolt. Always attach an endcap to the cut end of a new cable to prevent it from fraying.

Brake lever clamp

Pivot

Pivot

Cable barrel

Dust boot covering barrel adjuster

Cable housing

BRAKE LEVERS

Most mountain bike brake levers have a cable adjuster on them. By unscrewing the outer barrel you can increase the tension on the cable taking up any slack. This can be used to adjust the feel and amount of pull you require. Another adjuster is used to tighten the cable against the main brake body, preventing it from coming loose.

CABLE BARRELS

It is very important to lubricate the barrel at the end of the cables. This is the most common point of brake cable failure. It is generally caused by lack of lubricant, which causes the cable barrels to jam instead of pivot. The best way to prevent this is to use a thick water-repellant grease on the cable barrels. You normally access the barrel by reaching underneath the brake lever body.

CANTILEVER STUDS

Periodically remove the brake capilers and grease the cantilever studs. When removing a capiler, hold the complete mechanism together to keep the parts in the right order. Note which of the three settings the brake spring is slotted into. Once cleaned and regreased, use Loctite on the mounting bolt to prevent it from rattling loose.

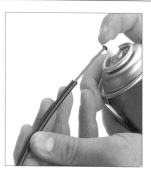

CABLE HOUSING

Keep the brake cable housing clean and free of kinks. Remove the inner cable from the housing and use a spray lubricant with a hose to flush out any dirt. Then put a thicker, Teflon-based lubricant inside the housing before reinstalling the inner cable. In wet conditions, inject a little grease into both ends to help stop dirt from getting in.

REMOVING RESIDUE

Clean the braking surface of the rim of the wheels regularly and rub down the surface of the brake pads with a light grade of wet-and-dry paper. This will remove the residue which can build up, and will improve the braking performance of the bike significantly.

Gears and chain

The nature of mountain biking means that the chain and gearing system are prone to a high rate of wear and tear. Most mountain bikes use indexed gear systems. These rely on all parts being accurately set up and in good working condition. If yours gives you problems, do not assume that it requires major new parts. Quite often it can be fixed relatively simply. There are also several steps you can take to make sure that your index system continues to work as smoothly as it did when you bought your bike.

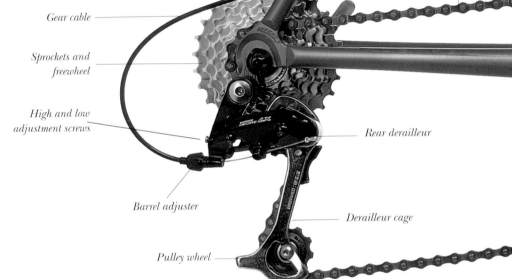

Chain

Gear cable

Sprockets and freewheel

High and low adjustment screws

Barrel adjuster

Rear derailleur

Derailleur cage

Pulley wheel

DIRTY CABLE HOUSING
It is common for water and grit to get into the rear cable housing. This affects both the derailleur and the index system. Take the cable out regularly and clean and lubricate it.

WORN SPROCKET
If your chain slips under pressure when it is on one of the smaller sprockets, you may have to replace the rear cassette or freewheel. Check for all the other possible problems before you do though, because their symptoms can be similar.

BENT DERAILLEUR HANGER
A bent hanger will throw out the synchronization of the gears. Remove the rear derailleur and use a large adjustable wrench to straighten it. Or, take it to a shop where they will have a specific tool for this job.

DAMAGED CHAIN
The most common problem that will cause the chain to jump is a stiff link. Most chain link extractors have a setting for removing stiff links. Alternatively, try pressing hard with your thumbs on either side of the rivet.

DIRTY CHAIN
An automatic chain cleaner is a good way to prolong the life of your chain and sprockets, and improve performance. It clips on and has a series of brushes that remove the grit and oil from the chain. Alternatively, use a toothbrush, solvent and tray.

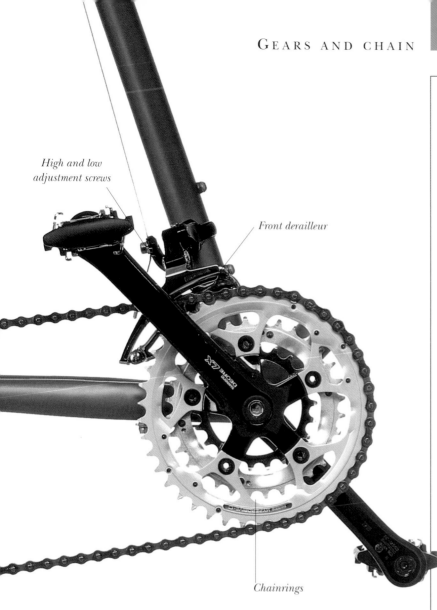

High and low adjustment screws

Front derailleur

Chainrings

Gears set up

CABLE TENSION

Index systems require regular tuning because of the precise nature of the mechanisms involved. The most important aspect of this tuning is getting the cable tension correct. If you have insufficient tension the derailleur action will be sluggish and will resist shifting the chain on the lower sprockets. If there is too much tension, the derailleur will overshift. It will also be sluggish on the downshift, preventing the chain from dropping down. An easy way to check the cable tension is to put the chain on the middle chainring and shift the rear derailleur on to the smaller sprocket. Feel the bare cable that goes to the rear derailleur. It should be quite taut. If it requires a small amount of adjustment, use the barrel adjuster (at the rear derailleur where the rear cable housing enters it) to fine tune it.

CABLE CONDITION

If your bike's gears seem to go in and out of tune from day to day, the cable probably needs replacing. The cable is a vital link between the shifter and the derailleur. It needs to have as smooth a path as possible. If it is kept clean and well lubricated, you shouldn't have any problems. Keep an eye open also for kinks in the cable because these will seriously hinder its performance.

DERAILLEUR CONDITION

To check for this, hold the rear derailleur by the bottom of the cage and try to move it from side to side. If you can feel definite play, it is likely that the bushings and bearings in the derailleur are worn. When a derailleur gets to this state the only option is to replace it.

FRONT DERAILLEUR

Check regularly that your front derailleur is adjusted correctly. The outer cage should sit exactly 1 mm above the outer chainring. The adjustment screws should be set so that the chain will travel across all three chainrings easily.

WORN CHAIN

Check the chain for wear, and change it if necessary. You can buy a specific tool for this, otherwise test by pulling the chain when it is on the outer chainring. If it comes away easily, you should replace it. A worn chain will also feel loose if you shake it.

Crankset and pedals

If you feel movement in either the cranks or pedals, and can hear creaks and clicks as you ride along, there is almost certainly something wrong with the crankset or pedals. The most common times that these parts get damaged are when they hit an obstacle, or when the bike is ridden when parts are loose. It is most important that you check all the bolts regularly and keep them done up tightly.

CHAINRINGS

If you bend a chainring on your mountain bike, providing it is not too badly bent, you will usually be able to straighten it. Bend it out carefully using an adjustable wrench slotted over the ring. Check the straightness by spinning the cranks backwards and using the front derailleur as a guide. If the ring is badly bent, you will have to replace it.

TIGHTENING THE BOLTS

The most important thing for you to check on the crankset and pedals is that all the mounting bolts are tight. These include the crank bolt and all the chainring bolts. Tighten the chainring bolts, with a good-quality Allen key and use Loctite on the threads. This will prevent them from rattling loose.

CRANK TAPERS

Most cranks fit on to a tapered square spindle. The crank and taper have precise edges, and if these are worn beyond a certain point, the crank will always come loose, no matter how tight the crank bolt is. Do not overtighten a crank because this will cause the taper on the crank arm to flare and make it impossible to tighten the crank.

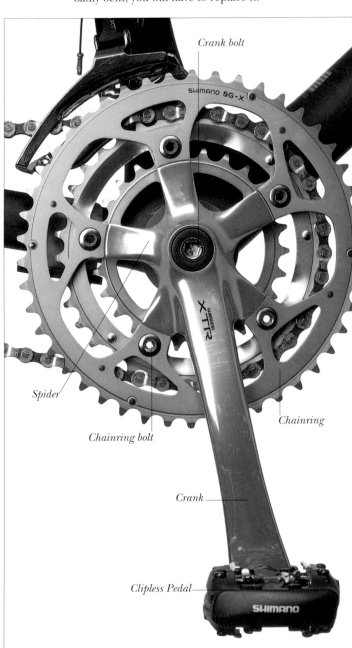

Crank bolt

SHIMANO SG-X

Spider

Chainring bolt

Chainring

Crank

Clipless Pedal

SHIMANO

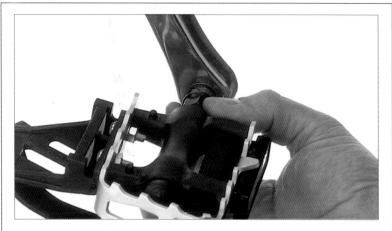

PEDAL BEARINGS

The surface of the pedal bearings is quite small, which can mean that they are not very smooth, and wear quickly. You can buy pedals with cartridge bearings which last significantly longer. When you replace pedals, always grease the threads before you screw them into the crank arm.

CLIPLESS PEDALS

The bearings in clipless pedals do not usually require as much maintenance as those in conventional pedals. Most clipless pedals have well-sealed cartridge bearings or ones that are enclosed. Keep the pedals clean and the springs well greased, and check regularly that all the small screws on the pedals are tight.

TOE CLIPS AND REFLECTORS

The bolts holding on the toe clips and pedal reflectors are notorious for working loose. Make sure they are tightly done up and ideally, replace normal nuts with nylock nuts that have a nylon insert which keeps them tight. This type of nut should also be used for mudguards and racks and any other bolt-on fitting that could become loose and cause a rattle.

CRANKS

If you have a loose crank, hold the bike frame and gently pull a crank arm outwards. If you get movement only on one side, it is likely that just one of your cranks is loose. If you see the other side moving, it is likely that the bottom bracket is loose. In both cases, get it repaired immediately.

CHAINRING TEETH

If you are having problems with the gears slipping under pressure, it is possible that the teeth on your chainrings are worn. A sign of this is that the

teeth will be very sharp and will slant steeply. If you buy new chainrings, check that they have the correct BCD (bolt circle diameter). There are many different sizes. If you are not sure, take the old chainring with you to the shop.

Front end

If you have a problem with any parts relating to the front end of your bike, such as the handlebars, stem, headset or forks, you will usually know quite quickly from the way the bike rides. You will feel if something is wrong through the handlebars. The classic things you will notice are severe vibrations when you brake, and the bike wanting to steer its own path.

Bar ends

Handlebars

A headset stem

Headset

Head tube

Suspension forks

HEADSET

If you ride on a loose headset you will feel a huge amount of vibration through the handlebars when you brake, which will make the bike difficult to control. You will also wear out the headset and can damage the frame beyond repair. The best way to check if the headset is loose is to pull the front brake and try to push the bike forwards. If it is loose you will have some play. To tighten it, loosen the top locknut first and then tighten the bottom one. Do not make it too tight. Check it by lifting the front wheel off the ground. The handlebars should turn smoothly and fall easily from side to side. Check for play again, then, when you have adjusted the bottom locknut to the correct position, hold the spanner on it and tighten the top locknut against it. You will know if your headset is worn because it will keep coming loose and will feel very rough when you rotate the bars from side to side.

STEM

If the front end of your bike creaks when you apply pressure to the handlebars, it is probably caused by a dirty stem. Undo the stem and pull it out. It should be greased but clean and not rusty. Also, undo the clamp and remove any grit from the bars.

HANDLEBARS AND BAR ENDS

Many mountain bikes have lightweight handlebars which can get bent during a crash or after several years' use. Look for small cracks going around the bars where they are clamped by the stem. If you see any, replace the handlebars. If you have bar ends, make sure that they are always done up firmly.

Rock Shox Judy suspension forks

AIR AND OIL SUSPENSION FORKS

The most common problem with air and oil suspension forks is a leak. You will normally be able to tell if air is leaking because the forks will feel sluggish and you may hear a slight hissing when they are compressed. With an oil leak, you will see a trickle of oil, normally coming out of one of the seals where the stanchion goes into the slider. If you have either of these leaks, take the forks to be repaired at an authorized service center.

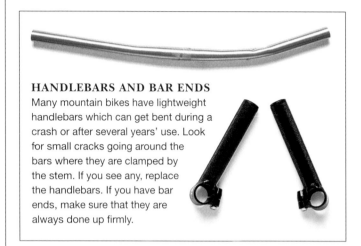

ELASTOMER SUSPENSION FORKS

Problems that can occur with elastomer forks are the forks seizing up and not moving at all, and the forks feeling mushy. If your forks seize up it is normally because water and grit have washed important grease out of the forks. Either take the forks apart yourself or take them to a service center to be cleaned and regreased. If your forks feel mushy, it normally means that the elastomer compound is worn out and needs replacing. This is a fairly simple job and can be done at home.

SUSPENSION FORKS

Even though suspension has given mountain bikers huge benefits, it is not without its problems. Suspension forks need to be kept clean, especially where the slider goes over the stanchion, otherwise the bearings will wear out. Worn bearings in suspension forks will give a similar feel to those of a loose headset. Suspension forks rely on lots of bolts for holding on the brace and crown. If you ever take these out, make sure that you use Loctite when refitting them. They must be tightened to the correct torque setting specified by the manufacturer. If they are not, it could result in major failure.

Wheels and tires

The parts of your bike that take more abuse than any other are the wheels and tires. The wheels take your weight and constantly get banged as you ride over obstacles and hard edges. At the same time the tires are pushed down on sharp stones and get rubbed against rocks, and take most of the braking and accelerating force.

SPOKES

Keep the spokes clean and occasionally put a drip of oil on both ends of each one. This will prevent the spokes from siezing in the nipples and will help them to pivot in the hub, reducing the chance of them breaking.

Spoke nipple

Rim

Hub

WHEEL RIMS

It is quite easy to dent the rim of a mountain bike wheel if you hit a hard edge or rock with great force. If it is a small dent, you can pull it straight with an adjustable wrench with a rag over it. If it is a big dent, you will have to get a new rim.

BRAKING SURFACES

Another common problem with rims is the braking surface being worn by the brake pads. A deep ridge will form all around the rim and when the tire is not inflated you may be able to flex the rim in your fingers. When this happens you must replace the rim.

TIRES

Check your tires for thorns, pieces of glass and wire. You are less likely to damage your rims and tires if the tires are kept pumped up to the correct pressure, as specified on the side. If you often get a puncture, check that the rim of the wheel does not have any sharp edges. Also check that the rim tape is properly installed, protecting the inner tube from the ends of any protruding spokes.

Sidewall

Tread

HUBS

Keep your hubs clean and well greased. Clean them by hand and check for play in the bearings at the same time. Do this by rotating the axle and trying to move it from side to side. If you have any play, get it tightened immediately.

HUB BEARINGS

Check that the bearings in the hubs are not worn by lifting the wheels off the ground in turn and spinning them. If you can feel a vibration going up through the handlebars it is likely that the bearings are worn.

TIRE TREAD

Check the state of the tire tread regularly. If it is worn down, it will have little traction and will be more likely to get a puncture. The rubber can perish after a time, in which case it will crumble when you rub it with a fingernail.

NEW TIRES

When putting on a new tire, check that the rim has rim tape on it. If it is difficult to get the tire over the rim, stretch the steel beading by standing on the tire with one foot and pulling the other side of the tire gently upwards.

TIRES AND BRAKES

When you have installed a new tire, check that the brakes clear the sidewall properly. You can tell if the pads are rubbing on the tire because you will hear a scuffing sound as the wheel touches them as it goes around.

CHAPTER 9

Extra information

Mountain biking has come a long way since it was 'invented' in the USA in the 1970s. As the sport has developed, the bikes have become more and more specialized, and some unique terminology has evolved too. If you want to enjoy the thrill of mountain biking to the fullest, you should understand the language, and learn a little about the sport's fascinating history. Many personalities have contributed to its development and played a part in making it as popular and accessible as it is today.

History of mountain biking

Since it began in 1977, mountain biking has raced to become a multi-million dollar industry, global activity and fully recognized sport. Its Californian pioneers, who once raced old bikes down dirt trails purely for kicks, are now millionaires and idols to a generation of enthusiasts.

1977

A group of cyclists in Northern California, in the United States, start to ride normal bikes off-road. They soon modify Schwinn beach-cruiser bikes to make the first basic mountain bikes. They add knobby tires, fit motorbike handlebars and brake levers, and reinforce the frames so that they will stand up to the rigors of off-road riding. To begin with they ride mostly downhill getting taken to the top in a truck. To make it possible to ride the bikes uphill, they later add derailleur gears which they take off their road racing bikes. (Some of these early pioneers, such as Gary Fisher, Tom Ritchey, Steve Potts, Joe Breeze and Charlie Kelly, are now mountain biking household names.)

1980

Suntour, the Japanese component manufacturer, makes the first specific mountain bike component group. This is a big step in mountain biking history because it will lead to bike manufacturers mass-producing mountain bikes.

Specialized, a small American wholesaler, creates the first production mountain bike called the Specialized Stump Jumper. This introduces mountain biking to a wider public.

1981

Mountain bike racing becomes increasingly popular with many events being staged around the United States. Most races are long out-and-back loops covering up to 50 miles.

The NORBA (National Off-Road Bicycle Association) Race Series for professional racers is set up and riders such as Joe Murray become the first professional mountain bikers.

1984

Shimano introduces the first Deore XT gruppo. This group sets new standards in mountain bike componentry and is still used as a bench-mark today.

Cannondale and Klein start to use aluminum for mountain bike tubing to make it lighter and stiffer. (Up until then, aluminum tubing had been used very little in the bicycle trade.) Cannondale and Klein do a lot of work with aluminum, testing it to its limits. (They still lead the way today in the production of aluminum for bikes.)

1989

John Tomac becomes the most successful mountain bike racer, earning the highest salary in the business. He wins the World Championship in both downhill and cross-country. His marketability as a racer gives him huge product endorsement fees and he is the first racer to recognize fully the importance of being successful on and off the bike. (Many of today's racers can thank him for the sponsorship fees they are paid.)

The Specialized Stump Jumper. The first production mountain bike.

1990

The first fully endorsed World Championship by the UCI (Union Cycliste Internationale) takes place in Durango, Colorado. This is a major step for mountain biking because up until now it has generally been snubbed by the international road racing fraternity. This brings in substantial sponsorship backing and means that the sport has a fully recognized world championship event. The initial events to get the rainbow jersey are the downhill and cross-country.

Paul Turner, an ex-moto-cross mechanic, develops and introduces the first suspension fork called Rock Shox. This is the first serious and well-executed form of bicycle suspension. It takes the world by storm and starts a suspension debate. A lot of people are critical of the forks at first, but most of them eventually take to riding on them.

1992

Many European racers cross over from professional road cycling to take up professional mountain bike contracts. They become a dominant force on the world mountain bike racing scene. This improves the image of mountain biking among cyclists worldwide.

Mountain bike frame geometry settles into having 71°-73° angles.

A battle starts between manufacturers to try to produce the ultimate suspension system.

1995

Grip Shift finally breaks the Shimano stronghold on gear shifter supply to bike manufacturers, with about 50 percent of manufacturers changing to Grip Shift. This increased competition should lead to the customer getting better value and better performance.

New suspension designs are constantly tested in the World Downhill Championship.

The world downhill speed record is set at 111 mph by the French rider, Christian Taillefer; Giovanna Bonazzi establishes a women's record of 89 mph.

1996

Mountain bike cross-country racing becomes a full fledged Olympic sport at the Olympic Games in Atlanta, Georgia.

Mountain biking A–Z

Italics indicate cross-referenced entries

A

Aheadset An alternative system to a conventional *headset* , which is lighter and easier to adjust.

air When a bike is in the air, as in 'getting big air' off a jump.

air and oil suspension forks *Suspension forks* that are air-sprung and oil-damped.

Allen bolt A type of bolt that is used on most bikes.

Allen key A tool which comes in various sizes and is used to do up or undo an *Allen bolt*.

anti-scam cam A device used to prevent the wheels or saddle from being stolen.

anti-seize A compound that is used to prevent two parts made of different materials from fusing together, for example, an aluminum *bottom bracket* cup and a steel frame.

axle The part on which the pedals, wheels or *hubs* revolve.

B

bar ends Extensions that can be added to the handlebars to give a greater variety of hand positions.

barrel adjuster A small device on brake levers and rear *derailleurs* to allow for fine-tuning of the *cables*.

BCD Bolt Circle Diameter. The spacing of bolt holes on *chainrings*.

bearings Small balls that rotate inside the *hubs, headset, bottom bracket,* and pedals to make these parts move easily.

blowout When an inner tube explodes suddenly with a bang, leaving a large hole.

BMX pedal A type of pedal that gives excellent grip and does not need *toe clips*.

bonding In manufacturing, a method of joining the tubes of a frame by gluing them together using a lug.

bottom bracket The *axle* and *bearing* assembly on to which the *cranks* are mounted.

bottom out When either a tire or *suspension* cannot absorb any more shock when you are riding a bike, and you feel a bang.

brake block The part of the brake that is in contact with the *rim*.

brake pad The rubber-like piece that slots into the *brake block*. Some brake blocks have replaceable pads.

brazing In manufacturing, a low-temperature method of joining tubes and attaching parts to a frame.

bunny hop A riding technique for getting over obstacles on the trail by lifting the whole bike clear of the ground.

bushings Small devices that reduce the friction between the moving parts of a *suspension*; also used with pulley wheels.

butting In manufacturing, a method of making a tube lighter and stronger by varying the wall thickness.

C

cable The steel wire that runs from the levers to activate the gears and brakes.

cable endcap The small metal sleeve that fits over the end of a cable to prevent it from fraying.

cable housing Plastic covering through which the cable runs from the gear and brake levers to fixed points on the frame.

cadence The speed at which you pedal. It is normally measured in revolutions per minute (rpm).

cantilever brakes The most widely used type of brake used on mountain bikes. They act on the *rim* by moving on a pivot.

carbon fiber A material with a high strength-to-weight ratio, which is used mainly for frames.

carcass The main body of the tire.

cartridge bearings A sealed *bearing* unit, which keeps out water and debris.

chain rivet The part that joins two chain links.

chainstay A frame tube that runs from the *bottom bracket* shell to the rear *dropout*.

chain suck When a chain gets jammed between either the *chainrings* or between the *crank* and the frame.

chainrings The front *sprockets*, which are mounted on to the *cranks*.

crankset All three *chainrings* and the *cranks*.

chromoly A steel alloy, which is used in producing most mountain bike frames.

cleat A small attachment on the bottom of a shoe, which interlocks with a *clipless pedal*.

clipless pedal A pedal that incorporates a system by which your shoe locks in and out of the pedal for more control, safety and efficiency.

Columbus An Italian manufacturer of fine-quality bike tubing.

composite wheel A wheel that is made of high-tech material such as *carbon fiber* and has no *spokes*, to make it stronger and more aerodynamic.

CPR tool A compact racing tool kit.

crank The arm that joins a pedal to the *bottom bracket*.

cross-country A type of racing that encompasses a wide variety of terrain.

D

dabbing A braking technique used to slow down quickly without skidding. <u>Also</u> putting a foot down during trials riding.

damper The part of a *suspension* system that controls the spring compression and extension.

derailleur The mechanism that pulls the chain from one *sprocket* to another.

disc brakes A powerful type of braking system, which uses large aluminum discs mounted on the *hubs* as the braking surface instead of the *rims*.

doubletrack A trail that is suitable for two bikes side by side.

down tube The tube on the frame that joins the *head tube* to the *bottom bracket* shell.

downhill A type of racing, over a course that goes only downhill.

drop-in When you ride off an edge and land on both wheels simultaneously.

drop-off When you ride off an edge down a near-vertical slope.

dropout The part where a wheel *axle* slots into the frame or *forks*.

E

Easton A high-tech manufacturer of high-quality aluminum tubing.

elastomer suspension forks A type of *suspension* system in which synthetic rubber is used for the springs and dampers.

entry-level bike A beginner's mountain bike at the bottom of the price range.

F

feathering A braking technique, which entails pulling the brake on and off several times to control speed.

flanges The two outer sections of the *hub*, to which the *spokes* are attached.

forks The two frame tubes that hold the front wheel.

frame size The measurement between the center of the *bottom bracket* axle to the center or top of the *seat tube*.

freehub The part of most cassette-type rear wheel hubs that allows the wheel to continue to turn when you stop pedalling.

freewheel An alternative to a *freehub*, in which the mechanism is attached to the *sprocket cluster* instead of the *hub*.

G

gear capacity The size of *sprockets* with which the *derailleur* is designed to cope.

gear ratio The relationship between the amount a rear *sprocket* turns and a *chainring* turns in a particular gear combination.

gel saddle A saddle that contains a soft compound, which molds to your shape, making the saddle more comfortable.

Grip Shift A gear shifter that works on a twist action.

Ground Control One of the best tires of all time, first manufactured in 1989.

group The standard components fitted to a bike, all produced by one manufacturer; gruppo.

gusset An added section of material which is put on to reinforce a particular area of the frame.

H

hanger The part of the frame on which the rear *derailleur* is mounted. <u>Also</u> A part through which the front and rear brakes are sometimes mounted, usually called the cable hanger.

head tube The tube that runs from the *forks* to the handlebar *stem*, containing the *headset*.

headset The *bearing* assembly in the *head tube* that enables you to steer smoothly, and which supports the *forks*.

high gear A gear you are in when the chain is on a small rear *sprocket* and a large *chainring*. You should be in a high gear when travelling fast downhill or on the flat.

hop-up A riding technique used for getting the bike over an obstacle by lifting the front wheel up and over it.

hub The center part of the wheel, which contains the *axle* and *bearings*, and to which the *spokes* are attached.

hydraulic brakes Fluid-operated brakes, which are far more powerful than conventional cable-operated brakes.

Hyperglide A type of *Shimano* rear *sprocket* and chain, which makes gear *shifting* under heavy loads easier.

I

Interglide An updated version of *Hyperglide*, with improved *shifting*.

index gearing A gear *shifting* system in which the gears click into place.

J

Judy (Rock Shox) Top-of-the-range suspension *forks*.

K

Klein, Gary The man who established aluminum as a viable alternative to steel as a frame material.

knobby A tire that gives excellent *traction* for *off-road* riding.

L

LED light A bright type of light, which uses Light Emitting Diodes instead of conventional bulbs.

line The route you take on your bike, for example when negotiating corners and rough terrain.

low gear A gear you are in when the chain is on a large rear *sprocket* and a small *chainring*. You should be in a low gear when riding uphill and over slow, technical terrain.

lube Oil or grease of various types used on the mechanical parts of the bike. (Short for lubricant.)

M

metal matrix A new type of super alloy used for frames, in which aluminum is mixed with particles of boron and ceramics.

mid-range bike A step up in quality and performance from an *entry-level bike*, in the middle of the price range.

monocoque A frame made in one large piece instead of from several tubes, making it stronger and lighter.

multi-tool A small tool incorporating several different tools.

O

off-road Any type of riding that is not on paved roads.

observed trials A type of competition in which riders have to negotiate a series of obstacles.

orienteering A type of race in which you have to find designated check points with the aid of a map.

Overend, Ned One of the first, and longest-competing, professional mountain bike racers.

P

Presta valve A type of valve on inner tubes, which gives excellent control of air pressure.

pro-racing bike A high-performance bike, which is suitable for professional racers to ride in competition.

PSI Pounds per Square Inch. A measurement of tire pressure.

pulley wheels The two small wheels in a rear *derailleur*.

R

reach The distance between the seat and the handlebars.

Reynolds A British manufacturer of high-quality steel tubing.

rim The outer part of a wheel to which the *spokes* are attached and on which the tire mounts.

Ritchey, Tom A pioneer of mountain biking.

Rock Shox A company started by Paul Turner, which made the first viable *suspension* system.

S

Schrader valve A type of valve used on mountain bike inner tubes, also on car and motorbike tires.

seat post The tube that attaches to the frame and the saddle.

seat stays The tubes that run from the rear *dropout* to where the *seat tube* meets the *top tube*.

seat tube The tube that runs from the *bottom bracket* shell to where the *seat post* is attached to the *top tube*.

setup The way in which a bike is arranged for a rider in terms of the position of all the adjustable components.

shifting Changing gear.

Shimano The largest manufacturer of bicycle components in the world.

sidewall The section of a tire between the *rim* and the *tread*.

singletrack A trail that is wide enough for only one bike.

slalom A type of race in which competitors have to ride in and out of a series of poles.

slick A type of tire with less tread, designed for riding on the road.

SPD Shimano Pedalling Dynamics. The *clipless pedal* system made by *Shimano*.

spokes The metal wires that connect the wheel *hub* to the *rim*.

spoke nipple The adjustable nut on a *spoke*, which holds the spoke in the *rim*.

spoking pattern The way the *spokes* are arranged in a wheel.

sprocket Any cog on a bike, eg. the rear sprockets, which are driven by the chain.

standover The amount of space between you and the *top tube* when you stand astride the bike.

STI Shimano Total Integration. A dual-control shifter that has two levers for gear *shifting* and incorporates a brake lever.

stem The tube assembly that connects the *forks* and the handlebars.

straddle wire The wire that links the two calipers of some *cantilever brakes*.

suspension A combination of springs and dampers installed on a bike, which improve the bike's handling, efficiency, rider safety and control.

suspension specific Any component that has been designed for use with a *suspension* bike, (e.g. a suspension front *hub*.)

T

tacoed A term used to describe a wheel that is so badly buckled that it looks like a taco chip.

Tange A tubing manufacturer which supplies most of the tubing used for bikes built in the Far East.

technical clothing Clothing that is designed in cut and fabric to be highly functional.

technical Referring to a section of trail that has challenging obstacles and terrain.

thumb shifters The original type of gear shifter which is operated with the thumb.

TIG welding Tungsten Inert Gas. The most commonly used method of frame building.

titanium A strong, light metal used in many top-level bikes.

toe clip A device attached to the pedal, which helps to keep your foot in position.

toe strap A strap used to keep your foot securely in a *toe clip*.

toe-in The angle at which the *brake pad* sits in relation to the *rim*.

top tube The tube that joins the *head tube* to the *seat tube*.

TPI Threads Per Inch. The number of nylon threads per square inch of fabric in a tire. A good-quality tire will have a high TPI, making it stronger, more durable, and more flexible.

traction The amount of grip a tire has on the ground.

trash To break a bike component.

tread The raised section of a tire which grips the ground.

Trek A major US mountain bike manufacturer.

True Temper A US manufactuer of steel tubing, which supplies most of the American market.

U

U-lock A large, strong bike padlock in the shape of a U.

W

wheel base The distance between the wheel *axles* of a bike.

wicking The ability of a fabric to take moisture away from your skin, to help prevent your body from overheating,

WTB Wilderness Trail Bikes. One of the founding companies of high-quality, high-performance mountain bike components.

Z

Z Max One of the all-time-best tires designed by *Tom Ritchey*.

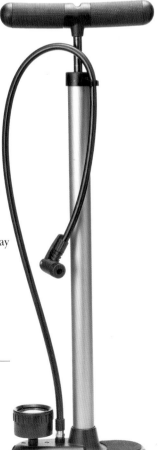

Index

Acknowledgments

Author's acknowledgments

I dedicate this book to my wife, Susanna, who gave her love and support throughout the project.

Thanks also to my business partner at Psycho, Jerry Wallis, who covered for me at the shop throughout our busiest time of the year. Also thanks to Alex, Pat, Steve and Dom for helping everything to run smoothly.

Finally a million thanks to Nick Fish at Trek UK, Ian Hughes at Scott UK, Chip Rimmer at Carratti Sport, Neil at Fishers of Finchley, Matthew and Cathy at Pace, Jerry and the team at Psycho, Rex Trimmell at X-lite and Jonathan and Ross at Southbank Cycles for use and supply of props. Thanks for everyone's patience and help.

Publisher's acknowledgments

The publisher would like to thank the following manufacturers and suppliers for kindly providing props for photography:

Bromley Bike Company: bike shop interior; **Carratti Sport**: GT bicycles, accessories and clothing; **Chartech**: Aqua3 waterproof maps; **Fishers of Finchley**: accessories and clothing; **Halfords**: Carrera bikes, helmets, accessories, child seats and bicycle racks; **Hope Technology**: disc brakes; **Olympus Sport**: Casual sports shoes; **Pace UK**: Pace bicycles; **Psycho**: bikes and accessories; **Scott UK**: Scott bicycles, accessories and clothing; **Serval Marketing**: Oakley sunglasses; **Sporting Image**: Sports footwear and clothes; **Southbank Cycles**: bikes and accessories; **Trek UK**: Trek bicycles, helmets, accessories and clothing; **X Lite**: bar ends and accessories.

The publisher would also like to thank:
Margaret Barnard, Rose and Helena Beer, Jill Behr, Paul Buckland, Emily Clowes, Finny Fox-Davies, Tom Fox-Davies, Dave Elliot, Emeka and Obi Ezekwo, Kate Gardener, Hazlegrove School, Terry Hardaker, Roger Healing, Dave Hermelin, Seb Kemp, Tony Kemp, Greg Morter, Dave Notley, Peter Parham, Lucy Pope, Laura Potts, Louise Pritchard, Derek Purdy, Celia Rahm, Jay Rawal, Rachel Rogers, Jason (Smokes) Sammuels, Charles Seaton, Pete Shoemark, Michelle Stevens, Anne Sushames, Nigel Tate, West Camel Farm and the Yeovil Cycle Centre.

Photographic credits
Key: t top, b bottom, l left, r right, m middle

Johns Bikes, Bath: 40; Emily Clowes: 142, 143; Dave Elliot / Exodus Travel: 125b, 131r, 132, 133, 136, 137; Malcolm Fearon: 125t; Hope Technology: 15tr; Matthew Oglethorpe: 141tr; Carlton Reid: 135t; Tim Ridley: 69 bl, bm, 147tr, br; Dave Stewart: 112bl, bm, 117, 120bl, 122bl, 123; Stockfile: 87tr, br, 112tr, 113tr, 114tl, 118, 119, 122tr, 124, 130, 134, 135b, 138, 139, 160; Trek UK: 116, 120br, 121; Tim Woodcock: 5, 129, 130.